Contents

C000053997

IMAGES OF WAR

THE FALL OF MALAYA AND SINGAPORE

RARE PHOTOGRAPHS FROM WARTIME ARCHIVES

Jon Diamond

Pen & Sword
MILITARY

First published in Great Britain in 2015 by
PEN & SWORD MILITARY
An imprint of
Pen & Sword Books Ltd
47 Church Street
Barnsley
South Yorkshire
S70 2AS

ISBN 978-1-47384-558-9

A CIP catalogue record for this book is available from the British Library.

Typeset by Concept, Huddersfield, West Yorkshire HD4 5JL.
Printed and bound in Malta by Gutenberg Press Ltd.

Pen & Sword Books Ltd incorporates the imprints of Pen & Sword Archaeology, Atlas, Aviation, Battleground, Discovery, Family History, History, Maritime, Military, Naval, Politics, Railways, Select, Social History, Transport, True Crime, and Claymore Press, Frontline Books, Leo Cooper, Praetorian Press, Remember When, Seaforth Publishing and Wharncliffe.

For a complete list of Pen & Sword titles please contact
PEN & SWORD BOOKS LIMITED
47 Church Street, Barnsley, South Yorkshire, S70 2AS, England
E-mail: enquiries@pen-and-sword.co.uk
Website: www.pen-and-sword.co.uk

Introduction

In 1941, Malaya was comprised of the Straits Settlements of Singapore, Malacca and Penang, which all formed a British colony under Governor Sir Shenton Thomas. Also included were the Federated States of Malaya, together with Perak, Selangor and Negri Sembilan. All were ostensibly ruled by a Federal government with its capital located at Kuala Lumpur. However, in many respects, each Federated State was self-governing and administered its own policy. In addition, there were also the Unfederated States of Johore, Trengganu, Kelantan, Kedah and Perlis, each governed by its own autocratic Sultan with a British adviser, and all incorporated into the British Empire by separate treaties. As governor of the Straits Settlements and high commissioner of both the Federated and Unfederated States, Sir Shenton Thomas frequently negotiated with eleven separate governments before any major policy affecting Malaya as a whole could be reached. This was a very cumbersome governing structure and, in a similar fashion, mimicked the British military command structure of Malaya and Singapore. Such a tangled hierarchy would make it difficult to both create and implement war plans as the peacetime days were rapidly fading in the late autumn of 1941.

The Malayan portion of the Malay Peninsula approximates 450 miles in the north-to-south direction. Malaya possesses a high north-to-south mountain range, which essentially bisects its portion of the peninsula that is shared with Thailand (see map, The Malaya Campaign, 8 December 1941–15 February 1942). This spine of jungle-covered hills, approximately 7,000 feet in the north and scaling down to 3,000 feet in the south, is flanked on both sides by coastal plains. The peninsula's western coast flanking the coastal plain has many mangrove swamps, while the eastern shore has many sandy beaches suitable for amphibious landings. Another topographic feature is that the peninsula has numerous east-to-west running rivers that intersect the eastern and western coastal plains. These waterways make their way from the mountains to the sea and are often filled with dense jungle and large areas of swamp. Heavy annual rainfall on the peninsula, over 250 inches in the mountains, allows for dense vegetation making the Malayan jungles thicker than Indian and Burmese counterparts, with battling mud always a problem. Some of these jungles and fields are almost impenetrable and visibility could be limited to a yard or two. On the western plain, though, and in the south at Johore, areas had been cleared extensively for cultivation of crops such as rice and tapioca as well as rubber tree plantation. This also meant that troops would have a much easier trek along the western coastal plain with its motor road trunk than on the eastern one.

The Malaya Campaign
8 Dec. 1941 – 15 Feb. 1942

THAILAND

South China Sea

Singora

Japanese V & XVIII Division landings on 8 Dec. 1941

Patani

Sadao

Japanese Takumi Force landing on 8 Dec. 1941

13 Dec. Jitra

Alor Star

Kota Bahru

Gong Kedah

Sungei Patani

Kroh

14 Dec.

Kuala Krai

George Town

Penang Is.

Butterworth

16 Dec.

Gerik

Selama

20 Dec.

18 Dec. Kuala Terengganu

Taiping

Port Weld

Kuala Kangsar

Ipoh

MALAYA

Dungan

Kuala Lipis

1 Jan.

Telok Anson

7 Jan.

Jernasang

31 Dec. Kuantan

3/4 Jan.

9 Jan.

Bentong

Maran

10 Dec. 1941 Prince of Wales & Repulse sunk

Selangor

Temerloh

9 Jan.

Kuala Lumpur

Port Swettenham

13 Jan.

Malacca Strait

Seremban

Gemas

Endau

Port Dickson

15 Jan.

Labis

26 Jan. Mersing

Malacca

16 Jan.

Muar

Kluang

Batu Pahat

SUMATRA

— Roads

—+— Railroads

⊗ RAF Airfields

➜ Axis of Japanese advance (with dates of Japanese occupation)

Johore Bahru

31 Jan.

⊙ Singapore

15 Feb. 1942

0   25   50   75 miles

0 25 50 75 kilometers

At the very tip of the Malay Peninsula, across the Straits of Johore, named after the Sultan of Johore, was Singapore Island, which was the epicentre of Britain's defensive plans in the Far East. Singapore is a wet low-lying island 85 miles north of the equator covering about 240 square miles with some of its coastline fringed by mangrove swamp. It extends 27 miles from east to west and 13 miles (at its maximal width) from north to south. The Straits of Johore, which separates the Malay Peninsula from Singapore Island, has a width that varies from 600 to 5,000 yards, and near the narrowest point the British constructed a causeway. Most of the coastline is coursed by creeks and small rivers. Most of the roads lead to Singapore City, located on the southern shore of the island towards its eastern end. In 1941, the island's population was approximately 550,000 inhabitants, comprised of Malays, Chinese, a few Tamils and Europeans, and most of the population lived in Singapore City. Except for scattered towns and settlements, the rest of the island was covered with rubber plantations and jungle growth.

The British High Command, as well as its political leaders, believed Singapore Island to be impregnable, as it had strongly fortified the southern and eastern coasts of the island with large calibre naval guns against seaborne assault. Singapore's main port was located at Keppel Harbour, which lies on the island's southern coast on the eastern end of the Malacca Straits, which separate Malaya and Singapore from the elongated island of Sumatra. It was not the 15-inch naval artillery guns of the Buona Vista and Johore batteries that concerned the Japanese High Command during their offensive strategy planning sessions in the autumn of 1941, but rather the fear that British Royal Air Force (RAF) and Royal Australian Air Force (RAAF) aircraft (with some Dutch Air Force aircrew as well) stationed on Singapore and at multiple airfields on the Malay Peninsula could interdict Japanese lines of communications (LOC), and potentially interfere with scheduled Imperial Japanese Army (IJA) offensives in resource-rich Sumatra and Java. Because of this geo-strategic position for Singapore, with numerous RAF and RAAF airfields, both Malaya and Singapore had to be captured before any subsequent operations against Java and Sumatra could be mounted.

After the carrier attack by the Imperial Japanese Navy (IJN) on Pearl Harbor, Hawaii, on 7 December 1941, the IJA conducted offensive operations across an incredibly broad front of 7,000 miles from Singapore to Midway Island. From early war planning sessions, Malaya and Singapore were targets for the IJA's major thrust while additional supporting operations were mounted to seize the Philippines, Guam, Hong Kong and parts of British Borneo in the Western Pacific. The Japanese High Command planned that once Malaya and Singapore were captured, these British bastions would serve as a springboard to seize southern Sumatra and an invasion of the Netherland East Indies (NEI) with its vast resources to supply Japan and its war effort, which had been occurring on the Asian mainland for almost a decade. Finally, southern Burma would be invaded with the intent of defeating the British and Indian forces there in order to sever the Burma Road and, thus, Chiang Kai-shek and his army's supply lifeline through the Burmese port of Rangoon. Ironically, the IJA utilized only eleven of its fifty-one divisions during these offensive operations in southern Asia, reserving the majority for home defence, continued offensives on the Chinese mainland and to possess a sufficient force in Manchuria to counter any possible Soviet moves against Japan there. This was to become, indeed, Imperial Japan's high-water mark.

In early January 1942, Field Marshal Sir Archibald Wavell was appointed supreme commander of ABDACOM, the cumbersome new combined American, British, Dutch and Australian Command to be headquartered in Bandung on Java after Churchill had designated him commander-in-chief (CIC) Far East on 30 December 1941. Wavell, as C-in-C, India, had previously noted about Singapore, before Pacific hostilities erupted, 'My impressions were that the whole atmosphere in Singapore was completely unwarlike, that they did not expect a Japanese attack and were very far from being keyed up to a war pitch.' This indifferent view was expressed by the local British military service commanders despite the vast Singapore naval base, which had been built at Sembawang on the north-east corner of the island after vociferous debate in the halls of Whitehall that had spanned years. The naval base was finally opened in 1938 and cost over £60m sterling. Its principal purpose was to serve as a deterrent to Japanese aggression against Britain's Far East colonies from Hong Kong and Malaya to the Antipodes.

The British High Command in London had envisioned that Singapore's 15-inch naval gun batteries of the Changi Fire Command on the east coast, covering the Johore River and eastern sea lanes through the South China Sea, as well as those at the Buona Vista overlooking Keppel Harbour, could sink any attacking enemy ship, while RAF and RAAF bombers and fighters, stationed along both coastlines of the Malay Peninsula after having been carved out of the Malayan jungle, would also deter any invading force. However, Singapore's naval base did not possess its own battle fleet moored at its docks. In the event of war, it was envisioned that the Royal Navy's battle fleet would sail through first the Suez Canal and then across the Indian Ocean and through the Malacca Strait to Singapore Island. In light of the anticipated lengthy Royal Navy sea voyage, if Japan attacked Malaya and Singapore, it was left to the RAF and RAAF to protect the relatively new naval base at Sembawang, while the British Army and its Commonwealth contingents were to protect the airfields on the Malay Peninsula. As events would soon demonstrate after the Japanese invasion of Malaya, the RAF and RAAF possessed too few frontline combat aircraft that could success- fully engage the far superior Japanese Army and Navy aircraft, and the British and Commonwealth forces were so undermanned and poorly trained for jungle combat and the aggressive Japanese jungle assault tactics that it could not even defend the paucity of planes stationed at those jungle airfields. Thus, Churchill committed only a token naval presence (Force *Z*) to Singapore, comprised of the modern battleship HMS *Prince of Wales* and the old battlecruiser HMS *Repulse* and four vintage destroyers (see Chapter Three for details) under the command of Admiral Sir Tom Phillips. There was no accompanying aircraft carrier for air cover against what would soon be the savage waves of Japan's twin-engine land-based naval bombers in the South China Sea and Gulf of Siam as the fleet aircraft carrier, HMS *Indomitable*, which was to join the two battleships, ran aground at Jamaica on 3 November 1941 and was in dry-dock for repairs. No other large carrier was available at the time.

On a brief visit to inspect Singapore's defences on 7 January, Wavell noted that there wasn't a single Allied tank in all of Malaya. This observation was made by the field marshal the day after fifteen Japanese tanks burst through the front lines of the 11th Indian Division and crossed the Slim River Bridge, which was only 250 air miles from Singapore. The military minds in London had concluded that tanks were unsuitable for jungle warfare. Also, Churchill was committing Britain's armoured forces to North Africa and Greece to combat the Italians and Germans rather than Singapore. In May 1941, this had become a major point of contention between the prime minister and his chief of the imperial general staff, General Sir John Dill, who favoured reinforcing Singapore with some armour. Also, Churchill was sending his new ally, the Soviet Union, Britain's older model infantry tanks (i.e. 'Matildas' and 'Valentines'), either of which would have been equal or superior to the Japanese armour that had landed on the Malay Peninsula and was making rapid southwards progress down the main trunk road on Malaya's west coast.

Therefore, while the respective staffs of the IJA and IJN were planning in the autumn of 1941 to invade and seize Malaya and Singapore in less than 100 days, the British service chiefs and civilian leaders were proposing a response to Japanese aggression that was fractured by both military and political concerns. The lack of consensus on the defenders' part was to prove highly inauspicious for the British Empire in the Far East after 7 December 1941.

Invading Japanese troops of the Twenty-fifth Army's 5th Division disembark from a barge with their equipment during an uncontested landing at Singora, Thailand on 8 December 1941. (*USAMHI*)

Japanese soldiers of the 18th IJA Division exit from their landing craft without opposition at Patani on Thailand's eastern coast on 8 December 1941. (*USAMHI*)

Japanese engineers attached to the invasion forces manually support a makeshift log bridge across one of Malaya's numerous waterways as was envisioned by Colonel Masanobu Tsuji of the Twenty-Fifth Army Headquarters. (USAMHI)

A British infantry section on patrol crosses a wooden pontoon bridge over a Malayan river. (USAMHI)

Japanese troops in heavy jungle camouflage infiltrating behind the enemy via a Malayan swampy area. These manoeuvres never-endingly caused havoc and panic among British and Commonwealth forces in Malaya who were usually road-bound. (*USAMHI*)

Mud was the ubiquitous enemy for both armies. Here Japanese troops pull one of their trucks out of Malayan earthen morass. (*USAMHI*)

Lieutenant Colonel Ian Stewart (*centre*), commanding officer of the Argyll and Sutherland Highlanders, marches through thick Malayan mangrove swamp mud to assess the difficulty of manoeuvring in such terrain. With him is Sergeant-Major Munnoch (*right*) and Major Angus MacDonald (*left*). (*USAMHI*)

A British infantry section marches through dense Malayan jungle. Not only did terrain necessitate an enormous amount of time to traverse but also many of the Allied troops were not properly acclimatized to it. Due to these factors, among others, Allied troops tended to confine themselves to roads and clearly marked trails whenever possible. (*USAMHI*)

In single file, troops of the 2nd Battalion of the Argyll and Sutherland Highlanders train in Malaya's dense vegetation. This body of British troops was considered the best trained at manoeuvring in difficult terrain. Here the individual soldier's head is barely visible above the tall grass. (*USAMHI*)

The 2nd Battalion of the Argyll and Sutherland Highlanders was one of the three British battalions mixed in with the brigades of the 11th Indian Division. Here, two are deployed with a machine-gun and a SMLE rifle in a Malayan rubber plantation. A 1927 Model Lanchester armoured car is in the background. (*USAMHI*)

Indian troops marching in column as part of their training along a Malayan road on the western coast of the peninsula. Unfortunately, during combat with the Japanese they were often outflanked because they preferred to stay on the roads. *(USAMHI)*

Japanese cyclists with heavy kit pedal down the main trunk on western side of Malay Peninsula. When the tyre rubber wore out, the Japanese soldiers kept riding their bicycles on the metal rims. *(USAMHI)*

The sultan's palace across the Straits of Johore in Johore Bahru from the Singapore side of the waterway. The Japanese occupied the palace using it as Lieutenant-General Yamashita's headquarters prior to Singapore's invasion. A breach in the causeway is evident below the tower, February 1942. (*USAMHI*)

RAAF over Malaya flying Lockheed Hudson bombers October 1941. These aircraft provided some useful aerial reconnaissance but were of limited value in stopping the Japanese onslaught with many aircraft destroyed on the ground in early air attacks after hostilities commenced. (*Library of Congress*)

RAF Catalina Flying Boats set out on patrol over Malayan coast before the war with their principal mission being aerial reconnaissance to locate an approaching hostile Japanese fleet. (*Library of Congress*)

Dutch Air Force pilots in Malaya go over a patrol plan prior to embarking on one of their missions. (*Library of Congress*)

(*Opposite page*) Japanese troops ashore watch from a high vantage point during a bombardment of enemy positions in early December 1941. (*USAMHI*)

Brewster Buffaloes of an RAAF squadron fly in the equatorial cumulus clouds over Malaya. (*Library of Congress*)

Field Marshal Wavell arrives at Batavia, NEI, for the ABDA Conference in early 1942. This combined American, British, Dutch and Australian command came into being on 3 January 1942. Wavell set up his HQ in Lembang in Java on 15 January 1942 in order to oversee all Allied forces in the Far East. The ABDA was disbanded on 22 February 1942 after Hong Kong, Singapore, Malaya and the NEI had all fallen. (*USAMHI*)

Wavell as ABDA commander meets with Americans Admiral Thomas Hart, commander of the Asiatic Fleet, and Lieutenant General George Brett, commander of United States Army Air Forces in Australia. The ABDA command was ludicrous since it encompassed all Allied forces in Burma, Singapore, Malaya, the NEI and the Philippines (of which Wavell never assumed control). (USAMHI)

General Sir Henry Pownall (left), who replaced Brooke-Popham as commander-in-chief Far East but shortly thereafter became the ABDA deputy commander. Here he tours Singapore's defences with Wavell (right) in January 1942. (USAMHI)

Singapore's long-awaited and expensive naval base under construction in 1938 at Sembawang adjacent to the Johore Strait at the extreme northern end of Singapore Island. (*USAMHI*)

One of Singapore's 15-inch naval guns. A battery of two guns was located at Buona Vista guarding the southern approaches to the island, while three guns comprised the Johore Battery on the island's eastern tip covering the Johore River and sea attack through the South China Sea. (*USAMHI*)

RAF personnel congregate on rubber plantations in northern Malaya before hostilities erupted. From here, the air and ground personnel would be relocated to one of the several airfields charged with interdicting any Japanese invasion. (*USAMHI*)

Japanese troops emerge from the Malayan jungle after having outflanked the road-bound British and Commonwealth forces. This manoeuvre worked repeatedly for Yamashita and his divisional commanders. (*USAMHI*)

Admiral Sir Tom Phillips, commander of Force Z, inspects Australian troops on Singapore Island. His task force of the HMS *Prince of Wales*, HMS *Repulse* and four destroyers lacked an aircraft carrier for suitable air cover. (*NARA*)

The Japanese Army commanders used combined infantry and light tanks to perfection during their advance through the Malayan jungle. The Allies were totally devoid of armour, having to rely almost exclusively on their 2-pounder anti-tank guns as their 25-pounder field guns were seldom used against the Japanese in an anti-tank role as was customary in North Africa. (*USAMHI*)

Japanese medium tanks advance down main trunk road in western Malaya. The Allies, except for rare occasions, used their ordnance effectively against Japanese armour. (*USAMHI*)

Air Chief Marshal Sir Robert Brooke-Popham (C-in-C Far East) (*left*), who was subsequently replaced by General Sir Henry Pownall, is seen here with Alfred Duff Cooper, Churchill's appointed Special Emissary in the Far East. The relationship between the military man and the civilian did not operate smoothly. (*USAMHI*)

Lieutenant-General Arthur Percival, who was considered very intelligent by his subordinates, seen here with Allied war correspondents on Singapore Island. Critics of Percival have claimed that he was a colourless character, more a staff officer than a commander and certainly not a natural leader. He did have difficulties inspiring confidence in his corps and divisional commanders, whether British or Australian. (*USAMHI*)

Chapter One

British Command Staff and Commonwealth Forces in Malaya and Singapore

On 15 February 1942, the island fortress of Singapore surrendered with its 85,000 men, not including the 45,000 that had previously surrendered on the Malayan Peninsula, thus ending one of the largest military disasters in the history of British arms since Cornwallis's capitulation to Franco-American forces at Yorktown in 1781 during America's revolutionary war. Lieutenant-General Arthur E. Percival's surrender to the invading Japanese Army permanently destroyed Britain's military and colonial prestige in the Far East. Since Percival sought out the best terms with the Japanese Army, thereby refusing to participate in any last stand heroics, he failed to meet Prime Minister Winston Churchill's standard as a consummate military commander. In mid-January 1942, Churchill had written to his chiefs of staff, upon receiving a report from Wavell that Singapore's northern coast was undefended, 'Not only must the defence of Singapore Island be maintained by every means, but the whole island must be fought for until every single unit and every single strong point has been separately destroyed. Finally, the city of Singapore must be converted into a citadel and defended to the death. No surrender can be contemplated.' Although humiliated in both photographs of the surrender ceremony and as a prisoner-of-war, analysis of Percival's pre-war assessment and plans for the defence of Singapore demonstrate that he was not entirely culpable for the Malayan and Singapore garrison's defeat. Poor planning of the defensive aspects of the island coupled with an under-equipped garrison to fight a modern battle with tanks and suitable aircraft ultimately may have been more causally related to the fortress's surrender than its army leadership. One must wonder whether Percival was a convenient scapegoat for a wider failure of British leadership and responsibility, both locally and at Whitehall.

As often is the case, however, the burden of responsibility falls on the shoulders of the battlefield commander. In support of this, Percival's chief engineer, Brigadier Ivan Simson, on Boxing Day, 26 December, pleaded with his commanding officer to build defence works on the northern shore of Singapore Island. To his dismay, Percival told him, 'Defences are bad for morale — both troops and civilian.' Almost exactly one month later Wavell visited Singapore and insisted that Percival erect defences on the northern shore. However, due to Wavell's underlying tacit personality, he did not impress the zeal and alacrity with which this defensive work needed to be completed. Up until a week before the Japanese crossed the Straits of Johore, no solid defensive works existed. A few of Singapore's 15-inch naval guns were directed north, but firing armour-piercing naval shells at Japanese troop positions on the very southern tip of the Malay Peninsula was futile.

Arthur Percival was born on 26 December 1887 in Hertfordshire, England. After schooling at Rugby he became a clerk for an iron mercantile company. When the First World War erupted, Percival enlisted as a private but was quickly promoted to second-lieutenant. Within three months he was again promoted to captain. Wounded during the Battle of the Somme, he was awarded the Military Cross. Further promotions ensued along with a Croix de Guerre and a Distinguished Service Order award. He was described in his confidential report as very efficient, beloved by his men, a brave soldier and recommended for staff college.

After the First World War, he served with the Archangel Command of the British Military Mission in 1919 in north Russia during the Russian Civil War. This was followed by a posting brutally fighting the Irish Republican Army (IRA) as an intelligence officer in 1920–21. It was during this service combating the IRA that brought him to the attention of Winston Churchill, then a cabinet minister, and Prime Minister David Lloyd George. Percival was selected as a student for the Staff College, Camberley, from 1923–24 upon a recommendation of Lloyd George. Thereafter, he served as a major for four years in the Royal West African Frontier Force in its colonial garrison as a staff officer culminating in a promotion to lieutenant-colonel in 1929. After studying at the Royal Naval College in 1930, he became an Instructor at the staff college in 1931–32. With the assistance of his mentor, General Sir John Dill, Percival commanded a battalion of the Cheshire Regiment from 1932–36, becoming a full colonel in 1936. Dill regarded Percival as an outstanding instructor and staff officer and wrote in his confidential report of 1932, 'He has not altogether an impressive presence and one may therefore fail, at first meeting him, to appreciate his sterling worth.' Dill recommended that Percival should attend the Imperial Defence College in 1935. In 1936, his mentor again helped Colonel Percival become the GSO 1 Malaya Command, serving as chief of staff to General William G.S. Dobbie, the General Officer Commanding (GOC) Malaya. In 1937, Percival returned home as a brigadier on the General Staff, Aldershot Command. However, it was during his posting with Dobbie that Percival made important observations about the defence of Singapore and conducted a detailed analysis about Singapore's vulnerabilities, not from the sea but from the Malay Peninsula. However, critics would cite that Percival had a 'gift for turning out neatly phrased, crisp memoranda on any subject [...] he was excellent in any job which did not involve contact with troops'.

From 1937–40, Dill enabled Percival to manoeuvre through a variety of staff and command positions, the latter including the 43rd (Wessex) and 44th Divisions. Then, as chief of the imperial general staff (CIGS), Dill appointed Percival GOC Malaya with the rank of lieutenant-general, promoted over the heads of many senior and more experienced officers, and he returned to Singapore on 15 May 1941. Dill's support of Percival was based on his evaluation of his protégé, who was an intelligent, efficient, tireless and professional staff officer. Critics of Percival have claimed that he was a colourless character, more a staff officer than a commander and certainly not a natural leader. Furthermore, it was asserted that he played everything by the rules, however ludicrous these might be, and if he did not lack urgency he certainly lacked passion. He was not a man for a crisis and certainly not a man for a desperate campaign. Ironically, when General Sir Alan Brooke was appointed CIGS replacing Dill, he reflected on such appointments that 'officers were being promoted to high command because they were proficient in staff work – which was quite wrong – and urged that fewer mistakes of this nature should be made in the future'. To exemplify Brooke's future concern, it had not helped Percival that in 1937 he had written an appreciation of the defence of Malaya and Singapore rather than holding an active command of British or Commonwealth troops in the field or combat. As CIGS, General Dill wanted more troops and armour sent to the Malaya command. However, Churchill would not acquiesce to this request, probably because of the need to reinforce the Middle East, which was then in heated combat with Rommel's *Deutches Afrika Korps* (DAK).

For over two decades the combined British military establishment pondered how to best defend Malaya and the Singapore naval base. Unfortunately, there was inter-service rivalry and often the RAF disdained to consult the army in regards to the placement of airfields along the Malay Peninsula. In 1937, Major-General William G.S. Dobbie, GOC Malaya, along with Percival as his chief of staff, looked at the problem of defence using the Japanese viewpoint as a new perspective. Percival and Dobbie had as an operational tenet that a British fleet could not arrive in less than seventy days (ironically the exact amount of time for Yamashita to conquer Malaya and Singapore) to carry out relief. The pair began conducting exercises with troops in October 1937 and reported that, contrary to the orthodox view, landings by the Japanese on the eastern seaboard of the peninsula were possible during the north-east monsoon from October to March, and this period was particularly dangerous because bad visibility would limit air reconnaissance. Both Dobbie and Percival warned that as a preliminary to their attack, the Japanese would probably establish advanced airfields in Thailand, and might also carry out landings along the coast of that country. If the appreciation composed by Percival, under Dobbie's oversight, was accepted, large reinforcements should have been sent without delay. Percival's appreciation was ignored. Furthermore, in July 1938, when Japanese intentions were more obvious, Dobbie warned that the jungle in Johore Province (i.e. southern Malaya) was not impassable to infantry, but again he was ignored.

By 1939, all Dobbie and Percival were able to wring out of the government was the small sum of £60,000, most of which was spent on building machine-gun emplacements along the southern shore of Singapore island and in Johore. Incredibly, the pre-war defence of northern Malaya was left in the hands of the Federated Malay States volunteers. A newly arrived Indian brigade group was held as a reserve for the defence of Johore Province. Singapore Island was entrusted to five regular battalions, two volunteer battalions, two coastal artillery regiments, three anti-aircraft regiments and four engineer fortress companies. The six air force squadrons had a total of fewer than 100 aircraft, including such venerable models as the Vicker Vildebeest biplane torpedo bomber, Hawker Harts and Audax biplanes. There were no tanks, which would prove important as the IJA would deploy armoured vehicles against British and Commonwealth defensive positions in the Malay States to the north of Singapore Island over and over again. The Argyll and Sutherland Highlanders had been issued with Bren carriers carrying the 0.55 inch Boys anti-tank rifle as well as Lanchester and Marmon-Herrington armoured cars, the former of which was obsolete and the latter rushed into production. The Lanchesters were built in 1927 and were equipped with two 7.7mm Vickers machine-guns and a 0.55-inch Boys anti-tank rifle. The South African-manufactured Marmon-Herrington vehicle, built in 1938, also had a Vickers 7.7mm machine-gun and a 0.55-inch Boys anti-tank rifle. The Boys anti-tank rifle had limited effect on the Japanese medium tanks while the Japanese 37mm tank gun was very adequate in piercing British armoured cars. For example the Marmon-Herrington had only 12mm of armour. It is no surprise that when Percival took up his new appointment, he had little enthusiasm or confidence. He wrote after the war, 'in going to Malaya I realized that there was the double danger either of being left in an inactive command for some years if war did not break out in the East or, if it did, of finding myself involved in a pretty sticky business with the inadequate forces.'

Upon his arrival, Percival discovered that the northern airstrips on the Malay Peninsula had not been situated in defensible positions nor did they have sufficient men or planes to occupy them, even though in August 1939, Air Vice-Marshal J.T. Babington, the local RAF commander, believed that Singapore was best defended by ensuring that Malaya remained in RAF hands and that the army should be deployed to defend the airfields. Many of his troops were in fact dispersed to guard the RAF's exposed airfields in northern Malaya. Percival deployed his three British and Indian Army divisions and three separate brigades in defensive positions near airfields, which was not too indifferent to Freyberg's defence of Crete with his New Zealanders, Australians and British troops in June 1941. The III Indian Corps, commanded by

General Sir Lewis Heath, who was knighted for his decisive victory over the Italians in Eritrea, was charged with the defence of northern Malaya with its 11th Indian Division deployed near the Thailand-Malayan border, under the command of Major-General David M. Murray-Lyon, while the 9th Indian Division was situated along the east coast of the Malay Peninsula. Construction of defence installations was stalled because of bureaucratic issues. Apart from a few regular British, Australian and Indian army battalions, the remaining troops were of mediocre or low-quality, under-trained and indifferently led. The reinforcements still on the way were no better and none had any idea of operating in the jungle. However, some units were well-led with a gallant tradition. The 2nd Battalion of Argyll and Sutherland Highlanders, under Lieutenant-Colonel Ian Stewart, arrived in August 1939, and turned out to be the best-trained British jungle fighters in Malaya, under Stewart's exercises and manoeuvres in dense vegetation, rubber plantations and mangrove swamps.

In fact, Dobbie's recommendations of 1937 were still a plan rather than a realized defensive framework to fend off a Japanese Army attack from the north. Some of the other service chiefs had held erroneous beliefs that their meagre resources and near-obsolete equipment would be sufficient to combat a battle-hardened Japanese war machine that was honed to a sharp edge after the conflict on the Chinese mainland for nearly a decade. Air Chief Marshal (ACM) Sir Robert Brooke-Popham, the commander-in-chief Far East, remarked incredulously, 'we can get on alright with (Brewster) Buffaloes out here [...] let England have the Super-Spitfires and Hyper-Hurricanes'. In fact, with most of the Royal Navy actively engaged fighting against the Germans, the British defensive plan focused on an aerial defence by 180 assorted aircraft operating from airfields on the Malay Peninsula and on Singapore Island. The Japanese, who had been in the planning stages of the invasion of Malaya, knew that RAF and RAAF aeroplane numbers were inflated for British propaganda purposes. Also, although thought by the Allies to be capable of defeating the Japanese aircraft that would oppose them, the Brewster F2A Buffalo was inferior in every respect to the Mitsubishi Zero except for armoured pilot and fuel protection.

In Percival's defence, he had too many political and logistical obstacles to overcome to make a meaningful contribution to the area's defence. First he tried to intensify training among his troops as well as obtain funding from the government to carry out defensive works. Second, he tried to construct defensive positions up north near the border with Thailand. However, local British business interests interfered, not wanting troops near their plantations or property. Finally, when a plan was formulated to attack and seize potential Japanese troop staging areas in Thailand, Operation *Matador*, both the detailed logistics and orders for advance were stalled. Percival had pondered that in the event of an imminent Japanese invasion through Thailand, the 11th Indian Division was to execute Operation *Matador*, which called for the occupation of Singora, several miles inside of Thailand, and its nearby airfields. From this key terrain the British could defeat, or at least delay, any Japanese advance. However, the British government's policy was to refrain from any act of provocation, bearing much similarity to the Phoney War on the Western Front prior to the Nazi onslaught in May 1940. Unfortunately for the British, because Operation *Matador* involved violating Thai neutrality, it was not politically feasible and thus never executed. This military vacillation continued until 6 December 1941, when it was known that the Japanese Army was en route to their staging areas in Thailand and their assault on the Malay Peninsula. Therefore, there was no realistic provision for a British attacking force to seize the Kra Isthmus in southern Thailand to prevent a Malay invasion by the Japanese until that country had clearly demonstrated itself to be the aggressor. In fact, it was Brooke-Popham who finally cancelled the plan whereby the 11th Indian Division would have entered Thailand to seize the Kra Isthmus. South of III Corps' area of responsibility, the 8th Australian Division was tasked to defend Johore Province, at the southern tip of the Malay Peninsula. An additional two infantry brigades were charged with the defence of Singapore Island proper, and a brigade remained in reserve. Because he had widely dispersed his divisions and brigades, General Percival was unable to concentrate his combat power at any one point until the Japanese had already overrun the peninsula. Royal Navy forces in Singapore, consisting of the recently arrived battleships HMS *Repulse* and HMS *Prince of Wales*, along with accompanying destroyers and cruisers, were located principally in Singapore, with the flexibility to attack either west or east, as the situation dictated. The fate of Task Force *Z* is discussed in Chapter Three.

At the command level, a vacuum of leadership developed at a crucial stage. ACM Brooke-Popham, C-in-C Far East, was replaced by Lieutenant-General Henry Pownall in November 1941. Pownall had served as Lord Gort's chief of staff with the British Expeditionary Force (BEF) in northern France and Belgium during the Phoney War and amid the disastrous retreat to Dunkirk. Pownall did not arrive in Singapore until 27 December, and then command was further altered with Field Marshal Sir Archibald Wavell being appointed to the American-British-Dutch-Australian (ABDA) command, with Pownall becoming his chief of staff. Thus, Percival's chain of command was initially more illusory than extant. In addition, one of Churchill's political allies, Duff Cooper, was appointed chairman of the Far East War Council. He had a fractious relationship with the local military leaders and departed for England after Wavell assumed the ABDA command in early January. At the subordinate level, Percival had difficulties with Lieutenant-General Sir Lewis Heath, commanding III Indian Corps, and Major-General H. Gordon Bennett, commanding the Australian troops in Malaya and Singapore. Heath's relations with Percival were acrimonious from the outset. Heath was more senior than Percival and had commanded the victorious 11th Indian Division in the Eritrean campaign under Wavell in 1940–41. After fighting commenced with Japan in northern Malaya, Percival lost confidence in Heath as III Corps

Commander, but did not sack him. Bennett was a bitter, outspoken subordinate. As an Australian army veteran of the First World War, he was prejudiced against the British military hierarchy. Furthermore, like all commanding Commonwealth officers, Bennett had the option to discuss orders from Percival with the Australian government if he disagreed with them, thus giving him considerable freedom of action. Bennett's view of Percival was that: 'he does not seem strong, rather the Yes man type. Listens a lot but says little [...] my estimate of him was right. Weak and hesitant though brainy.' Although Percival had the opportunity to sack Bennett as well, he allowed him to continue commanding the Australian contingent. Finally, the relationship between Bennett and Heath was, to say the least, irascible. The recipe for disaster at Percival's command level was complete.

As Percival noted after the war, his appreciation made in 1937, under Dobbie's auspices, did not differ from that adopted by the Japanese when they attacked Malaya in December 1941. Percival also claimed that when he had joined Dill at Aldershot in 1938, he had warned him that Singapore was 'far from being impregnable and would be in imminent danger if war broke out in the Far East'. As a case in point, Singapore Island's 15-inch batteries numbered only two and were located on the southern side (Buona Vista Battery, two guns) and in the north-east corner (Johore Battery, just due south of Changi, three guns), covering the Johore River and South China Sea to the north-east). The island possessed two batteries of 9.2-inch guns: the Connaught Battery on Pulau Blankang Mati, south of Keppel Harbour, and the Tekong Besar Battery on the island of that name to the north-east of Singapore Island. In addition, there were nine batteries of 6-inch guns scattered across Singapore Island. However, it is worth noting that there were no naval gun batteries along the entire northern coast of Singapore Island, despite the expensive naval base being located there at Sembawang. Some have speculated that, after having composed the appreciation about Malaya and Singapore's defence in 1937, Percival's outlook about the likelihood of repelling a Japanese invasion was quite realistic rather than being pessimistic.

Although the chiefs of staff in August 1940 recommended reinforcing Malaya and Singapore, Churchill vehemently objected. The prime minister's overriding concern was combating the Italians in the Mediterranean and Middle East, where he knew it to be the only theatre in which he could actively combat Axis forces at that time. It must be remembered that the epic struggle between the RAF and the Luftwaffe was in full height at this time and the British Isles were bracing for a Nazi invasion just two months after the debacle at Dunkirk. It may well be that the prime minister was incorrect on a number of different levels. First, Japanese military assets had always been undervalued by the Western democracies. Second, the presence of HMS *Prince of Wales* and HMS *Repulse* was, by no means, a satisfactory replacement for a large British fleet with aircraft carrier fighter protection, nor could it deter Japanese aggressive movements long enough for additional vessels to arrive. As for the ongoing training and supply of equipment of British and Commonwealth troops, shipments of Lend-Lease military ordnance from the United States as well as armaments from Britain continued to arrive at Singapore for assembly and transport to Malaya as well as troop arrival, training and transfer of air assets and pilots from Singapore Island to Malayan airfields. Finally, Churchill had already decided to have the United States guarantee the safety of British garrisons in the Far East. However, America was waiting for Japan to act as the aggressor before taking an active military stance.

Percival and staff officers march to the Ford factory at Bukit Timah accompanied by Japanese Staff Officer Sugita to enter into formal surrender negotiations with the Japanese 25th Army Commander, Lieutenant-General Yamashita. (NARA)

British troops erecting only southern beach obstacles to stop Japanese landing craft at certain tidal levels on Singapore Island, December 1941. Defensive works on the northern shore facing Johore Bahru were considered bad for civilian morale by the commanding British general, Lieutenant-General Arthur Percival. (*USAMHI*)

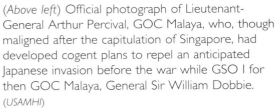

(*Above left*) Official photograph of Lieutenant-General Arthur Percival, GOC Malaya, who, though maligned after the capitulation of Singapore, had developed cogent plans to repel an anticipated Japanese invasion before the war while GSO I for then GOC Malaya, General Sir William Dobbie. (*USAMHI*)

(*Above right*) Field Marshal Archibald Wavell, appointed to lead the ABDA Command on 3 January 1942, inspects a 15-inch naval gun emplacement with subordinates on Singapore Island in January 1942. Two such batteries were present at Buono Vista on the southern coast and the Johore Battery on the island's eastern tip. (*USAMHI*)

(*Right*) General Sir William Dobbie, GOC Malaya 1937. Together with his GSO I, Colonel Percival, this pair of British officers conducted a prescient detailed analysis about Singapore's vulnerabilities not from the sea but from a Japanese seaborne invasion of the Malay Peninsula using neutral Thailand's eastern beaches as an initial staging point. (*USAMHI*)

(*Above left*) Field Marshal Sir John Dill (*centre*) was Percival's mentor and later CIGS prior to the outbreak of war in the Far East. Churchill ended his tenure as CIGS in December 1941, in large part due to a dispute over Dill's written comments of May 1941 to strengthen Singapore's defences with armour and other tools of war at the expense of the Middle East theatre and possibility of losing Cairo. Dill then became Churchill's chief of the British joint staff mission (JSM) as well as the senior British member on the combined chiefs of staff (CCS) in Washington, DC, where he developed a close working and personal relationship with US Army chief of staff, General George C. Marshall (*right*). Here both are seen reviewing troops at the United State Army Infantry School, Fort Benning, Georgia. School Commandant General Leven C. Allen is saluting (*left background*). (*USAMHI*)

(*Above right*) Lieutenant General Percival (*right*), GOC Malaya, Field Marshal Wavell, C-in-C India, and soon-to-be-appointed ABDA commander (*centre*), and Air Chief Marshal Sir Robert Brooke-Popham C-in-C Far East (awaiting General Pownall as his replacement) (*left*) at Singapore HQ in December 1941. (*USAMHI*)

British soldiers in camouflaged solar topees man a Vickers machine-gun in an attempt to strengthen Singapore Island's southern shore defences before the war. (*Library of Congress*)

Federated Malay States Regiment at bayonet practice. Relatively inexperienced troops such as these were to counter any anticipated Japanese invasion of northern Malaya. (*USAMHI*)

Federated Malay States Regiment troops during field exercises before the war to heighten their preparation for the anticipated conflict with Japan. (*USAMHI*)

Indian troops line-up after landing at Singapore to reinforce the Johore Province garrison in southern Malaya. (*NARA*)

Argyll and Sutherland Highlanders on training march in Johore Province to get acclimatized to the equatorial conditions of southern Malaya. (*Library of Congress*)

British troops arrive in Singapore before the war with their solar topees and much enthusiasm. (*USAMHI*)

Argyll and Sutherland Highlanders rest after training in Mersing, Johore Province before the war. The fatigue they exhibit was due in large part to the harsh equatorial heat and humidity. (*USAMHI*).

Straits Settlement Volunteer Force (SSVF) set out on a training march. This detail was going to set up mines. Note the second soldier from the left is carrying a Very flare pistol. *(USAMHI)*

Indian Anti-Aircraft Artillery (AAA) battery at Singapore prepares to insert a shell into the breach of a 3.7-inch AAA gun. The British Army in all theatres failed to seriously employ this excellent weapon in an anti-tank role like the vaunted German 88mm gun. *(USAMHI)*

Indian Bren gun team using the weapon as an anti-aircraft one on Singapore. Although very accurate as an infantry section's support weapon, the Bren's limited magazine capacity clearly limited sustained fire in an anti-aircraft role. (*USAMHI*)

British universal carriers training in Malayan dense vegetation. The one shown here is armed with a Bren light machine-gun and a Boys 0.55 inch anti-tank (AT) rifle, which proved ineffective against Japanese medium tanks. The Boys AT rifle became obsolete soon after its debut in 1937. (*USAMHI*)

Argyll and Sutherland Highlander jumps from his Lanchester armoured car in Malaya with a Vickers Mk. I medium machine-gun with a front bipod and rear monopod mounted on. The Vickers Mk. I gun fired the same .303 inch calibre cartridge as the lighter machine-guns such as the Bren gun, as well as the standard issue SMLE rifle. As a result of its water cooling it was exceptionally suited for continuous firing. The other Highlander to the *right* is getting the water can and ammunition box ready. (*Library of Congress*)

Major-Generals H.G. Bennett, C-in-C Australian troops in Malaya and Singapore and D.M. Murray-Lyon, GOC 11th Indian Division of III Corps. Both commanders had a fractious relationship with Percival. (*USAMHI*)

Australian 22nd Brigade disembarks at Singapore 18 February 1941. The 22nd Brigade would bear the brunt of the main Japanese assault on Singapore Island almost a year to the date of their arrival. (*AWM*)

Wavell, as C-in-C India, inspecting soldiers of the 2nd Gordon Highlanders in Singapore in November 1941. To the left of Wavell in the photograph is ACM Sir Robert Brooke-Popham, C-in-C Far East. (*Author's collection*)

Here, 9th Gurkha Regiment soldiers train with 3 inch mortar in Malayan jungle. Along with the 25-pounder field artillery piece, this weapon was quite effective in disrupting massed Japanese infantry assaults. (*Library of Congress*)

Officers and NCOs of the 2nd Battalion of the Argyll and Sutherland Highlanders at a briefing on a rubber plantation in Malaya. This was the backbone of the battalion that had superbly trained the Highlanders for jungle warfare. (*Library of Congress*)

(*Opposite page*) Indian troops of the Dogra Regiment training in the Malayan jungle. The sergeant leading this section of soldiers has a map folder in his left hand and an encased compass hanging from his neck. (*Library of Congress*)

Brewster Buffalo fighters of Australian 454 Squadron RAAF lined-up wingtip to wingtip for this photograph. Although the pilot had armour protection, this fighter, which was the United State Navy's first monoplane fighter in 1938, was outclassed by both the IJA's 'Nate' and Oscar fighters as well as the IJN's Zero. (*AWM*)

(*Above left*) Air Chief Marshal Sir Robert Brooke-Popham, C-in-C Far East, who dithered about ordering Operation *Matador* into effect, such that the Japanese landed unopposed on the Thai beaches of Singora and Patani. (*USAMHI*)

(*Above centre*) General Sir Henry Pownall took over as C-in-C Far East from Air Chief Marshal Brooke-Popham in November 1941, but arrived at Singapore in late December. He had previously been Lord Gort's chief of staff during the German *blitzkrieg* in May 1940, resulting in the evacuation at Dunkirk. After only a few days as C-in-C Far East, he stepped aside to become Wavell's chief of staff when the latter assumed the ABDA Command in early January 1942, which incorporated the Far East Command. (*USAMHI*)

(*Above right*) Lieutenant-General Sir Lewis Heath, III Indian Corps commander, who was knighted after his victories over the Duke of Aosta's Italian Army in Eritrea, while leading the 11th Indian Division there during January – April, 1941. (*USAMHI*)

(*Right*) Lieutenant-General Percival and Major-General H. Gordon Bennett, GOC Australian troops in Malaya pose for a photograph in Singapore. In addition to Bennett's prerogative to contact his home government if he questioned Percival's orders, he also worked closely with Wavell on a plan to defend Johore Province, which was contrary to Percival's strategy. Their military relationship was a cantankerous one. (*USAMHI*)

Lend-Lease material to aid the British arriving at Singapore's Keppel Harbour from the United States before Pearl Harbor when the Americans were neutral but supplying arms and munitions to Britain, then the only Western democracy combating Germany and Italy. After Pearl Harbor, the United States would become an active belligerent against the Axis forces in both the Pacific and Europe. (*Library of Congress*)

Here, 25-pounder field artillery pieces with their Quad tractors and ammunition limbers embark at Keppel Harbour on Singapore Island for a rail journey to the Malayan Peninsula. Without tanks these guns would be the most formidable weapons among the British and Commonwealth ground forces. (*Library of Congress*)

(*Above*) Lanchester armoured cars ready for transport from Singapore to the Malayan Peninsula. Earlier models of these armoured cars served in the First World War with these later ones being produced in 1927. By 1939, most Lanchesters were sent to the Far East and assigned to the Selangor and Perak battalions of the Federated Malay States Volunteer Force as well as the 2nd Battalion of the Argyll and Sutherland Highlanders in Malaya. The main armament of the vehicle included a .50 calibre Vickers machine-gun and two other .303 calibre Vickers machine-guns, the latter ones in a dual mount. Their thin armour of 9mm made them easy prey for Japanese light and medium tanks and, although they had good cross-country performance, they were too big, heavy and slow for reconnaissance missions. (*Library of Congress*)

(*Opposite above*) The Bristol Blenheim Mk. IV Long Nose bombers arrive at Singapore for assembly. In this model, the forward fuselage was revised and lengthened by 3 feet to include a navigator's station under a glazed upper surface with a downward-scalloped port side. The Blenheim Mk. IV equipped one squadron in the Far East. (*Library of Congress*)

(*Opposite below*) Here, 25-pounder field artillery pieces are being transported on railcars in Singapore for their final destination on the Malayan Peninsula. (*Library of Congress*)

Indian soldier flashes a victory sign from a porthole on a troopship arriving at Singapore's Keppel Harbour.
(*Library of Congress*)

Indian troops boarding a train to depart Singapore Island for their new garrisons on the Malayan Peninsula. Many of the reinforcements lacked sufficient battle experience like the 11th Indian Division that had served in Eritrea during Wavell's East Africa campaign of January until May 1941.
(*Library of Congress*)

British troops pose in tropical kit upon arrival to Singapore's Keppel Harbour. After arriving in Singapore, a lot of time was required for acclimatization to the equatorial environment.
(*Author's collection*)

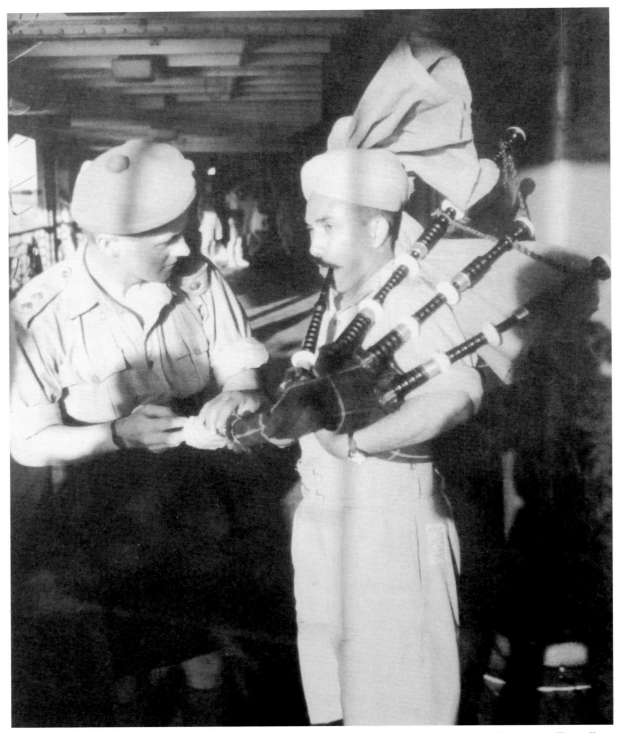

Scottish officer teaches Indian soldier how to play the bagpipes aboard a troopship bound for Singapore. The officer is wearing his traditional kilt and demonstrates the polyglot nature of the British and Commonwealth forces in Malaya and Singapore. (*Library of Congress*)

British troops in tropical kit standing at ease with their camouflaged solar topees in Malaya before the outbreak of hostilities. Members of this infantry section are armed with SMLE rifles, while an NCO carries his Thompson submachine-gun at ease. They are practising the rudiments of camouflage and concealment in the jungle. (*Author's collection*)

A platoon from the 9th Gurkha Regiment is seen advancing during Malayan manoeuvres before the war. The NCO (*far right*) kneels with his Thompson submachine-gun while the soldier behind him next to the tree rests his Bren light-machine-gun on its bipod. (*Library of Congress*)

A pair of 9th Gurkhas training in a cautious, slow advance against an enemy position with the soldier in the foreground lying prone. Both Gurkhas have their fearsome 18-inch sword bayonets attached to their SMLE rifles in the Malayan jungle before the Japanese invasion. (*Library of Congress*)

A Gurkha warrant officer giving map directions to his NCOs in the Malayan jungle during field exercises in preparation for the anticipated outbreak of war with Japan. (*Library of Congress*)

A section of camouflaged British infantry troops training in the dense Malayan vegetation. The section's NCO is carrying a Thompson submachine-gun with a drum magazine, while the other soldiers have the standard issue SMLE rifle. *(Library of Congress)*

Elements of a British platoon practice charging with fixed bayonets on their SMLE rifles while their NCOs (*front row*) have Thompson submachine-guns. The soldier in the *left rear* is carrying his Bren light-machine-gun. *(Library of Congress)*

A camouflaged soldier of the 1st Battalion Manchester Regiment, which had previously seen action against Arab insurgents in Palestine before the war, leans against a tree to better aim his shot using a SMLE rifle. (*Library of Congress*)

British troops train in deploying barbed wire for a roadblock as they unload some from a lorry on a Malayan road.
(*Library of Congress*)

One British soldier helps another fasten his webbing while on training manoeuvres in dense Malayan vegetation.
(*Library of Congress*)

Indian soldiers of the Dogra Regiment practising with rubber boats on a lake near Singapore. (*Library of Congress*)

A British soldier helps load another drum onto a Lewis machine-gun positioned on its front bipod while on a training exercise on Malaya in 1941. This venerable weapon of First World War vintage was designed by an American and used .303 inch ammunition while being operated by gas and air cooling. It was one of the first infantry support weapons to be widely deployed. (*Author's collection*)

Malay troops training using a smoke screen to conceal their attack on Malaya. (*USAMHI*)

A crewman of a 2nd Argyll and Sutherland Highlander Lanchester armoured car sends a hand signal while on manoeuvres before the war. (*Library of Congress*)

(*Opposite page*) Indian troops with an impromptu bipod for Bren gun prepare during an air-raid drill. The limited number of rounds per magazine made the Bren light-machine-gun very ineffective with sustained fire at rapid flying aircraft. (*USAMHI*)

Australian troops march before the Sultan Abdul Samad's palace before the war. (*Library of Congress*)

Indian soldiers of the Dogra Regiment train on a lake near Singapore in a variety of watercraft and are assisted by a British soldier lending his cane to help land the boat.
(*Library of Congress*)

Indian soldiers practice with 3-inch mortars in Malaya. These mortars were used frequently due to a lack of adequate artillery support against the Japanese infantry advance. (*Library of Congress*)

Indian gunners practice loading their field artillery piece in a Malayan rubber plantation. Note how the soldier at the *right* has opened the breach and is waiting for the round to be loaded. *(Library of Congress)*

Field Marshal Wavell (*far left*) inspects Indian mortar section on one of his visits to Singapore as C-in-C India just before the war in November 1941. To the right of Wavell is Air Chief Marshal Sir Robert Brooke-Popham, C-in-C Far East, in the solar topee. *(Author's collection)*

(*Above*) Indian soldiers embark onto a wooden boat tied to a pier in southern Johore Province during an invasion exercise. (*USAMHI*)

(*Opposite above*) Indian mountain artillery battery gunners train on a rubber plantation in Malaya. (*USAMHI*)

(*Opposite below*) Bristol Blenheim Mk.I bomber over Tengah Airfield on Singapore Island *en route* to its new base at Alor Star in north-western Malaya's Kedah Province south of the Thai border during the first few days of December 1941. All but one of the bombers in the squadron would eventually be destroyed by repeated Japanese air attacks commencing on 8 December 1941. (*AWM*)

Catalina flying boat lies still with a relaxed crew on the aircraft's wings and engines before its preparation to take off in Malayan waters to patrol Indian Ocean and South China Sea before the Japanese attack. (*AWM*)

Tamil helpers assist in the launch of a Catalina flying boat down the slipway for an aerial reconnaissance patrol mission from Singapore. (*Library of Congress*)

RAF pilot gears up before take off from a Malayan airfield. The RAF and RAAF antiquated fighters were no match for the Japanese III Air Division's Zero fighters or the IJA Oscars and Nates. (*AWM*)

Lieutenant-General Arthur Percival with Averill Harriman, President Roosevelt's emissary to Britain at Sembawang Airfield, just south of the naval base, on Singapore Island before the war in the Pacific started. Part of Harriman's position was to evaluate the efficiency with which Lend-Lease supplies were arriving to Britain and its overseas garrisons. (*USAMHI*)

Chapter Two

The Japanese Invasion Plan and Assault

During 1941, as the American embargo on Japan was intensified, Malaya was sought after as a great prize by the Japanese High Command. Apart from Malaya's production of approximately 40 per cent of the world's rubber and 58 per cent of its tin, capturing the great British naval base at Singapore would open up the entire area for further invasions and acquisitions. The Japanese already knew that Singapore Fortress was practically defenceless facing northwards towards Johore, RAF and RAAF fighter strength was exaggerated for propaganda purposes, and although there were five to six divisions of the British Army stationed in Malaya, totalling about 80,000 troops, less than 50 per cent were British.

The Japanese invasion plan, utilizing the 25th Japanese Army, under the command of Lieutenant-General Tomoyuki Yamashita, and comprised of three crack Japanese infantry divisions, the 5th, 18th and Imperial Guards Division, was to concentrate on the RAF and RAAF airfields in northern Malaya during the initial stages. The plan for each of the three divisions was strictly mapped out. The IJA 5th Division with a tank regiment's support would land at Singora and Patani, both harbours with beaches on Thailand's east coast, just north of the Thailand-Malaya border, and then rapidly drive south across Thailand's border into western Malaya. The aim of this advance was to capture the Kedah Province airfields along the north-western Malayan coast in the vicinity of Jitra, Aloe Star and Butterworth, and then cross the Perak River into Perak Province. Then, the IJA 5th Division was to continue southwards and capture Kuala Lumpur, the capital of Malaya's Federated States. The 18th Division's 56th Regiment, also known as the Takumi Force (after its commander Major-General Takumi), was to land on the north-eastern Malay coast near the key northern airfield of Kota Bahru, just south of the Thai border, capturing the airfields there. Colonel Masanobu Tsuji, Chief of Operations and Planning Staff, 25th Japanese Army, believed that RAF and RAAF aircraft stationed in the vicinity of Kota Bahru particularly threatened the landings at Singora and Patani to the north. The 56th Regiment was then to trek southwards along Malaya's eastern coast to Kuantan and capture its airfield there. Another regiment from this Chrysanthemum Division was to seize British Borneo while the third regiment landed at Singora-Patani as a reserve for the IJA invasion operation. The Imperial Guards Division would land later at Singora, or another port to be selected, and follow the 5th IJA Division into Malaya to become part of the 25th Army's reserve after it assisted in the seizure of Thailand and the start of the Burmese invasion. Once the advance south was proceeding, these two divisions would occupy the main trunk road down Malaya's west coast and head southwards. The 18th IJA Division would operate along the eastern coast of the Malay Peninsula.

The Japanese intended to first neutralize the threat of the RAF and RAAF in Malaya with over 500 of its aircraft from the Japanese 3rd Air Division, and then allow this air armada to provide the necessary tactical air support against Commonwealth forces on the peninsula. The IJN's second fleet provided the amphibious arm to the landing operations and then surface support as needed. The Japanese wanted the conquest of Malaya and Singapore to occur in less than 100 days before significant British and Commonwealth reinforcements could reach the island or peninsula.

The Japanese fighters, both of the army and navy, were vastly superior to the RAF and RAAF Brewster Buffaloes. The Ki-43 Oscar (Hayabusa, meaning peregrine falcon to the Japanese), was a formidable aircraft being considered the Japanese Army's best fighter in terms of lightness, manoeuvrability and speed. The Ki-43 was developed in 1937 when the Japanese Army decided to produce a fighter with a retractable undercarriage to succeed the Ki-27. This newer fighter went into service in June 1941. The Oscar was armed with only two 12.7 machine-guns and it had no pilot armour, self-sealing fuel tanks or starter motor until later in the war. This fighter proved very successful against Allied aircraft early in the war despite its light armament. After encounters with more advanced Allied fighters, later in the war armour and self-sealing fuel tanks were added. The Ki-43 was deployed in greater numbers than any other Imperial Army fighter and was second only to the Imperial Japanese Navy's Zero in terms of sheer numbers in the air armamentarium. The A6M Mitsubishi Reisen was known to the Allies as the Zero or Zeke. It was the Japanese Navy's main and superb fighter aircraft in all Pacific theatres and was the first carrier-borne aircraft in the world to achieve full parity with its land-based contemporaries. When fitted with a drop tank, the Zero had a phenomenal range and had superior armament to the Oscar with its two 20mm fixed forward-firing cannon in the leading edges of the wing and two 7.7mm forward-firing machine-guns in the forward fuselage.

The Brewster F2A Buffalo was ordered as the US Navy's first monoplane fighter, the prototype of which appeared in 1938 and entered service in July 1939. The Buffalo Mk.I was delivered by the United States to both the British in Malaya and the Dutch in the NEI. The Brewster Buffalo was outmoded by the time of the Japanese invasion and had not taken part in either the European or North African theatres because it was superseded by faster, more efficient fighters. It was certainly outperformed by either the Japanese Army's Oscar or Japanese Navy's Zero, even though the Japanese did suffer several planes shot down by Allied aircraft and ground fire.

As planning for the invasion and capture of Malaya and Singapore began in earnest three months before the assault, attention to potential problems with such an invasion and the solutions needed were tackled quickly. For example, after a survey of the topography and infrastructure of Malaya was made, it was noted that there were no less than 250 bridges along the main trunk road between Singapore and the Thai border due to the many east-to-west running rivers. Japanese logisticians, principally among them Colonel Tsuji based at a jungle warfare training centre on Formosa, realized that the longer it took to repair destroyed bridges, the longer the British would have to build up their defences in Johore Province and Singapore Island. Therefore, it was decided that an entire engineer regiment (for bridge reconstruction) should be allocated to each of the three divisions in the 25th Japanese Army and a fourth one under the army commander General Yamashita's direct control.

Lieutenant-General Yamashita was appointed commander of the 25th Japanese Army on 5 November 1941. Although respected by many of his peers, the newly-installed Prime Minister Tojo was an enemy of his and attempted to keep him out of Tokyo and the seat of power. Another enemy was his immediate superior, General Terauchi, commander of the Southern Army. Thus, when recalled as the army commander in Manchuko in northern China to lead the 25th Japanese Army's invasion of Malaya and Singapore, Yamashita knew about his perilous political position and how only a quick and decisive victory could protect him from demotion, or worse. Two of the three division commanders of the 25th Japanese Army had good relationships with Yamashita and also possessed vast experience in opposed landings during the Sino-Japanese War. They were Lieutenant-General Matsui, commander of the 5th IJA Division, and Lieutenant-General Renya Mutaguchi, commander of the elite 18th or Chrysanthemum IJA Division. The third division, the Imperial Guards Division, had as its commander Lieutenant-General Nishimura, who was another old enemy of Yamashita. Ancillary units supporting the three IJA divisions were two regiments of heavy field artillery and the III Tank Brigade. The total strength of the 25th Japanese Army was 60,000 men. Yamashita was also to be supported by the 3rd Air Division with approximately 450 aircraft and the IJN's fleet air wing contributing an additional sixty aircraft.

At Singora and Patani, the 5th Division's landings commenced on 8 December 1941 at 0400 hours, which was just over an hour after the Pearl Harbor raid. It was unopposed by Thai forces. However, the 56th Infantry Regiment's landing on the eastern Malay coast at Kota Bahru was strongly opposed by British forces just a few hours later that day. With the IJN surface fleet lending naval gunfire, this regiment broke through the British brigade defending the coastline in close order combat with bayonet charges, which were typical of IJA training doctrine. However, the price to pay for pressing these attacks on the British positions at Kota Bahru was steep. By midnight of 8 December, the airfield at Kota Bahru was firmly in Japanese possession and the Japanese troops re-grouped after the heavy fighting following the amphibious assault.

The Japanese aircraft that occupied the airfields at Singora and Patani, on Thailand's east coast, destroyed sixty of the 100 British aircraft in northern Malaya by 9 December, gaining total air domination by the end of the fourth day of the invasion. The British plan was already beginning to shatter. From the start the Japanese had kept the British off balance in Malaya. Outnumbered more than two to one, the Japanese, never hesitating to re-group or re-supply their forces, surged down the main roads on the western side of the peninsula on thousands of bicycles and in hundreds of abandoned British cars and trucks. Because of Malaya's intense heat, the bicycles' tires blew out. However, the resourceful Japanese learned to ride down the paved motor road trunk on the rims of the bicycles. The sound of metal to pavement sounded like tanks and the peninsula's defenders, notably the relatively inexperienced Indian troops who were terrified of armour, often broke for the rear.

Lieutenant-General Tomoyuki Yamashita, 25th Army Commander, who both politically and militarily needed a speedy conquest over Malaya and Singapore. After his victory he acquired the sobriquet Tiger of Malaya. (USAMHI)

Lieutenant-General Takuro Matsui, Commander of the IJA 5th Division, enjoyed an excellent relationship with Yamashita. His division was highly mechanized and experienced from service in China. (USAMHI)

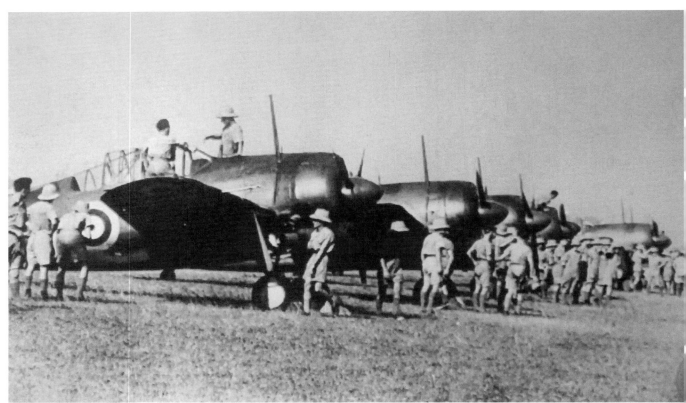

RAF ground personnel with American-built Brewster Buffalo fighters at a northern Malayan airfield. Because of its shape, this fighter was pejoratively dubbed the 'Flying Barrel'. (*Author's collection*)

RAAF pilots with their Lockheed Hudson Mk. IVA bombers, which were acquired from the United States via Lend-Lease, at a northern Malayan airfield. In addition to its six .303-inch machine-guns and an internal bomb-load of 1,350lb, the Hudson (along with the Catalina flying boat) was instrumental for coast reconnaissance. (*AWM*)

A squadron of RAAF Brewster Buffaloes flies in formation over Malaya. Due to their slower speed and less manoeuvrability, they were no match for their contemporary Japanese counterparts. *(Library of Congress)*

Japanese troops in captured fishing boat appear cheerful as they prepare for their unopposed landing at Patani, Thailand on 8 December 1941. *(USAMHI)*

Japanese troops leisurely landing their equipment from a small craft at Singora, Thailand. (*USAMHI*)

(*Opposite page*) Japanese infantry settle on board an assault barge off Thailand's eastern coast for their uncontested assault on Singora on 8 December 1941. (*USAMHI*)

A Japanese Special Naval Landing Force, or *Rikusentai*, officer leads his troops ashore without opposition along Thailand's coast. The IJN had no marine corps as such, but members of ships' companies were chosen to act as landing parties when required. (*USAMHI*)

Japanese 5th Division infantrymen land
unopposed on Singora beach, 8 December
1941. (USAMHI)

Lieutenant-General Renya Mutaguchi,
18th Division commander. He had served in
China with Yamashita and they were on
excellent terms. Mutaguchi would go on to
command this same division, as well as the
Japanese 15th Army, in Burma and for the
invasion of Assam, India in 1944. (USAMHI)

Colonel Masanobu Tsuji, the main Japanese logistician on Yamashita's 25th Army Staff for the Malaya attack. He created manuals for jungle fighting and insisted on having an engineer regiment with each of the three invading IJA divisions to rebuild damaged bridges. (*USAMHI*)

Japanese assault troops from Mutaguchi's 56th Regiment (Takumi Force) board a landing barge to attack north-eastern Malaya's Kota Bahru, just south of the Thai border, on 8 December 1941. (*USAMHI*)

Two Nakajima Ki-43 Hayabusa Oscar army fighters prepare for a mission on the Malayan Peninsula in early December 1941. This plane was the most advanced fighter available to the IJA in the opening phases of the Second World War and came as a very considerable shock to the Allied air forces. (*USAMHI*)

A trio of Nakajima Ki-43 Hayabusa Oscar army fighters patrols overhead after having won air supremacy of the RAF and RAAF in December 1941. (*USAMHI*)

(*Opposite page*) Work crews assemble American-built Brewster Buffaloes in a Singapore hangar for transfer to northern and eastern Malayan airfields. On a few occasions, these planes and their pilots meted out some punishment to the Japanese air forces. However, the reverse was usually the case. (*Library of Congress*)

A Japanese Army pilot climbs into his Nakajima Ki-43 Hayabusa Oscar army fighter for a mission over the Malayan Peninsula in December 1941. (*USAMHI*)

A Japanese pilot lies dead after being shot down over Malaya by British anti-aircraft artillery. (*USAMHI*)

A Japanese soldier views a captured British anti-aircraft artillery that is fixed to its platform in a well-constructed gun pit. (*USAMHI*)

Japanese troops beside their diminutive Type 92 tankettes, which were armed with a single 7.7mm Type 97 machine-guns, come ashore on the Malayan Peninsula. (*USAMHI*)

(*Above left*) Japanese engineers manhandle a bridge section into place to repair a damaged crossing in Malaya. Colonel Tsuji had anticipated such difficulties in his planning the operation a few months before the invasion. (*USAMHI*)

(*Above right*) Heavily laden Japanese troops, some with bicycles, cross a wooden log improvised bridge. The engineers in the background are stripped of their clothes to keep them dry. (*USAMHI*)

(*Opposite page*) Japanese engineers build a new bridge over a Malayan jungle waterway with wooden beams and planks. (*USAMHI*)

Japanese troops haul a field artillery piece up a steep jungle embankment in the Malayan jungle. *(USAMHI)*

Camouflaged Japanese gunners move their Type 92 battalion Howitzer into position. *(USAMHI)*

The 25th Army commander, General Yamashita, reviews map co-ordinates with his subordinates during the advance down the Malayan Peninsula. (*USAMHI*)

A British pillbox at Kota Bahru. The Japanese were heavily confronted by the British and their fortifications in their defence of this north-eastern Malayan coastal position causing significant Japanese casualties in the initial assault waves. (*USAMHI*)

Japanese soldiers lie dead by the tide's edge near their 49-foot Type A landing barge (*Daisatsu*), which was the most common one used by the IJA. It could carry 100–120 men, ten horses, an artillery piece or a light tank. (*USAMHI*)

A Japanese officer with his sword drawn leads his troops in an assault on British forces at Kota Bahru on 8 December 1941. (*USAMHI*)

A Japanese infantryman fires his Arisaka 6.5mm Type 38 rifle. A longer 7.7mm variant was also produced but the shorter one was more useful in jungle terrain. (*USAMHI*)

(*Above*) A Japanese infantry group, armed with a flamethrower, attacks an enemy pillbox. These British entrenchments strongly contested the initial Japanese landings at Kota Bahru with deadly machine-gunfire on assaulting troops leaving their barges. (*USAMHI*)

(*Right*) Japanese assault troops with their highly successful light infantry support weapon, the knee mortar, which could hurl a grenade 75 yards. The Japanese soldier (*left*) holds the grenades in his hands. (*USAMHI*)

(*Opposite page*) Japanese troops with bayonets fixed and helmets camouflaged use stealth as a tactic while warily approaching an enemy position in dense vegetation. (*USAMHI*)

Japanese soldiers pose in a martial stance with their bayonets fixed and helmets donning vegetation as camouflage. *(USAMHI)*

Lying in the prone position, awaiting the order to commence an assault, a Japanese soldier fixes his bayonet to his Arisaka rifle. The Japanese were heavily instructed on using the bayonet as a major infantry weapon at their training depots. *(USAMHI)*

Japanese troops preparing for a bayonet charge. Often the soldiers would tie a family inscribed banner to the end of their Arisaka rifle for good fortune. (*USAMHI*)

Japanese troops charging through a Malayan rubber tree plantation. Direct bayonet assaults and stealthy outflanking were typical infantry manoeuvres that unnerved the British and Commonwealth troops defending Malaya. (*USAMHI*)

(*Above*) Japanese troops, using portable filtering devices, purify Malayan jungle water sources. Waiting for supplies and reinforcements was not part of the Japanese plan as they relentlessly pushed down the peninsula. (*USAMHI*)

(*Opposite above*) A Japanese flamethrower assists infantry in their assault on enemy slit trenches and earthen fortifications. Very often the retreating British and Commonwealth forces had too little time to prepare extensive defence works to meet the Japanese who were pressing their attack. (*USAMHI*)

(*Opposite below*) Japanese soldiers lay dead in dense Malayan growth victims of their reckless but effective style of assault on enemy positions. The 25th Army commander, Yamashita, enforced a very strict time agenda, less than a hundred days, in capturing the peninsula and Singapore Island. (*USAMHI*)

(*Left*) Three Japanese ground personnel prepare their Nakajima Hayabusa Ki-43 Oscar for a mission. A bomb is suspended from the forward fuselage. The Allied air forces learned in a bitter way how versatile this IJA fighter was. (*USAMHI*)

(*Opposite page*) Japanese troops find some time for rest in their intense campaign for Malaya. The capture of Malaya and Singapore took Yamashita's forces just under seventy days. (*USAMHI*)

(*Below*) British civilian cars and trucks were abandoned in Malaya by the droves after the December 1941 invasion. The Japanese not only used these vehicles to their advantage down the Malayan Peninsula but after the capitulation shipped many to New Guinea for use on the Papuan Front. (*USAMHI*)

Japanese troops ride on or walk beside their bicycles. The troops walking are exercising different muscles to give the individual infantryman more endurance for the advance. (USAMHI)

A Japanese soldier carries his loaded bicycle over a log bridge. His full kit attached to the rear and front fenders could weigh as much as 60lb. (USAMHI)

Japanese troops walking beside their bicycles to rest certain muscle groups during the advance down the western Malayan road trunk. In addition to capturing the north-western Malayan airfields, the IJA 5th Division's axis of advance was to get to this road trunk on the western side of the peninsula to expedite the southward advance towards Singapore Island. (*USAMHI*)

Japanese Type 95 light tanks with a 37mm gun on the turret and two 7.7mm machine-guns advance past captured civilian vehicles down the Malayan trunk road on the western side of the island. Certain members of the British High Command before the war had concluded that tanks were not suitable for operation in Malaya, which was clearly a lethal mistake. (USAMHI)

Chapter Three

Royal Navy Disaster in the Gulf of Siam

The sinking of HMS *Prince of Wales* and HMS *Repulse* was a seminal naval engagement in the Second World War, which illustrated the effectiveness of aerial attacks against naval forces that were not adequately protected by air cover and the resulting importance of including an aircraft carrier in any major fleet action. The British High Command had decided to seek out and sink the Japanese invasion fleet to counter the heavy losses already incurred in northern Malaya in early December 1941. Force Z was comprised of the new 35,000-ton British King George V class battleship HMS *Prince of Wales* (under the command of Captain John C. Leach) and the older 32,000-ton battle cruiser HMS *Repulse* (under the command of Captain William George Tennant). Force Z was under the command of Rear Admiral Sir Tom Spencer Vaughan Phillips, who was aboard HMS *Prince of Wales*, and sortied, without air cover as the RAF and RAAF were now eliminated as threats in north-eastern Malaya, to counterattack the Japanese fleet. Phillips was sceptical that battleships could be sunk by aircraft, as had been demonstrated by the American aviator Billy Mitchell several years earlier. On 10 December, the IJN Air Force's land-based, twin-engine Mitsubishi G4M Betty and Mitsubishi G3M Nell medium attack planes of the 22nd Air Flotilla, functioning as both high-level bombers and sea-level torpedo-bearing aircraft, from their base in Saigon, sank both capital ships east of Malaya, near Kuantan, effectively rendering the Commonwealth and British Army without naval support in addition to the destruction of the RAF and RAAF forces in Malaya a couple of days earlier.

Phillips was regarded by Winston Churchill, then first lord of the admiralty, as one of the Royal Navy's highest intellects. Phillips' last action was in 1915. By the time Britain was combating Germany during the Second World War, Phillips was deputy chief of naval staff. He had taken over the job from Admiral Andrew Cunningham, who had left to command the Mediterranean Fleet. Cunningham, a man of action, considered Phillips to have been promoted above his talents. Nonetheless, Phillips interacted quite well with Churchill. Other British admirals, though, clashed with Phillips. When confronted by fellow Admiral Sir John Tovey, commander-in-chief of the Home fleet, about the need for air cover for ships at sea, Phillips became irate and virtually accused Tovey of being a coward. Phillips was quoted as saying that 'bombers are no match for battleships'. He was renowned for his impatience with those sailors who believed in naval air power, while Tovey had been against sending HMS *Prince of Wales* to the Orient as it would leave the Home fleet with only one modern battleship to counter the German surface fleet desperately trying to sever the tenuous Atlantic convoy lifeline from North America.

Captain Leach's career was noteworthy for his involvement during the stalking and sinking of the German battleship *Bismarck* in late May 1941, in which an obsolete Fairey Swordfish biplane from the British carrier HMS *Ark Royal* had its torpedo strike the stern of the German battleship causing its rudder to jam, thereby preventing its passage to safety at Brest. The *Bismarck*, like Force Z, lacked air cover, so Captain Leach knew first-hand of his ship's potential vulnerability from aerial attack. Captain Tennant earned military praise when he led the Royal Navy's shore party in orchestrating the evacuation of the BEF off the beaches of Dunkirk in June 1940 and personally saw the *Luftwaffe's* destruction of surface ships, despite the presence of the RAF.

The original British plan had called for a larger fleet, which included the new Illustrious-class aircraft carrier HMS *Indomitable* for air cover. The plan had to be revised when HMS *Indomitable* was damaged *en route*, after running aground in the British West Indies. Ultimately, it was Churchill's decision to allocate HMS *Prince of Wales* and HMS *Repulse* to Singapore's defence, without the initially intended air cover, in October 1941 to deter expansionist Japan from entering the war. However, it was only a token compromise to demonstrate how the British needed to protect its various colonial territories in Malaya, Borneo and the Straits Settlements. The British prime minister assured the Commonwealth prime ministers, 'In my view, *Prince of Wales* will be the best possible deterrent' to Japanese aggression.

It is ironic that it was the British, who had invented the aircraft carrier during the First World War, but were still reluctant two decades later to fully grasp the vulnerability of surface vessels from aerial attack. Furthermore, this disaster for the Royal Navy occurred just over a year after the Mediterranean fleet's brilliant attack on Italian battleships at Taranto in November 1940, by carrier-based Fairey Swordfish torpedo bombers flying at less than 150 miles per hour at sea level. Parenthetically, it was the Taranto attack that served as a blueprint for the Japanese Navy's plan to attack the United States' Pacific Fleet at Pearl Harbor in 1941. Also, German planes, especially the slower Stuka dive bombers, destroyed numerous British warships without air cover off Crete, in May 1941, that were attempting to both reinforce and evacuate the island.

HMS *Prince of Wales* was commissioned in 1941 and as armament formidably possessed ten 14-inch guns, four twin 5.25-inch dual-purpose (anti-ship or anti-aircraft) guns, six sets of eight-barrelled 2-pounder pom-poms, a 40mm Bofors gun, and a number of 20mm Oerlikon light cannons and Lewis machine-guns. The admiralty believed that this ship had the most modern design and weaponry for comprehensive protection from either torpedo or aerial bomb attack given the fact that HMS *Prince of Wales* was well-equipped with horizontal armour. HMS *Repulse* was commissioned in August 1916 and as her main armament carried six 15-inch guns and nine 4-inch guns. Her anti-aircraft armament was of limited quantity and was composed of just six hand-operated, high-angle 4-inch guns and three sets of eight-barrelled 2-pounder pom-poms. HMS *Repulse* was also an older ship and in 1941 was deficient in the horizontal armour needed for protection against aerial bombardment. Force Z arrived at Singapore Harbour on 2 December 1941 to a triumphant and jubilant reception, just days before the IJN attack on Pearl Harbor on 7 December and the start of the IJA invasion of Malaya the following day. For the inhabitants and military command at Singapore, it was a welcome reinforcement, especially since the considerable armaments of the two capital ships strengthened the two 15-inch shore gun batteries that formed Singapore's main defence on its southern (Buono Vista battery) and eastern (Johore battery) coasts. To Admiral Phillips' credit, he did request Hawker Hurricanes for land-based air cover;. However, he was informed that none of these fighters were available. The RAF could offer only a combat-untested squadron of the much slower, under-gunned Brewster Buffalo fighters piloted by the Australians. These now-obsolete planes were no match for the much-vaunted Japanese Navy and Army fighters.

On 6 December, reports were received in Singapore of a Japanese invasion fleet off the south coast of Indochina, and HMS *Repulse* and two destroyers, which were on a training cruise to Port Darwin, were hastily recalled back to their new base. Force Z, along with four escorting destroyers, HMS *Express*, HMS *Electra*, HMS *Tenedos* and the Australian vessel *Vampire*, sortied from Singapore during the early evening hours of 8 December. After intelligence reported that a Japanese invasion fleet was advancing on the northern Malayan Peninsula, Admiral Phillips devised a plan to launch a surprise surface attack against it off Kota Bahru, but he could not even count on Malayan-based RAF or RAAF cover since those airfields were already in the process of being overrun in northern Malaya. Instead, Phillips requested planes from Singapore to provide air reconnaissance to the north of his intended target at Kota Bahru and fighter cover over Singora. Phillips intended to strike at the enemy as they landed their forces, hoping to sever their supply lines and give the British troops ashore the chance to throw the invaders back into the sea.

The next day, 9 December, during the afternoon, Phillips received a message from Singapore categorically stating that fighter cover over Singora was not possible. Admiral Phillips was also unaware that Japanese Vice-Admiral Takeo Kurita's invasion fleet had two battleships escorting the thirty troop transports. In addition, his invasion fleet could count on approximately 100 bombers, forty fighters and six air reconnaissance planes of the 22nd Air Flotilla stationed at Saigon in French Indochina. Concealed by rain and clouds over the Gulf of Siam, HMS *Prince of Wales* and HMS *Repulse* were sighted by the Japanese submarine *I-65* (later to be re-numbered *I-165*) at 1345 hours. There was some signals interference, initially from that submarine. However, within two hours, IJN headquarters in Saigon received the submarine's message giving the composition of the British task force, its speed and direction. Later that afternoon, the British fleet believed it had been sighted by three Japanese reconnaissance planes in the Gulf of Siam. In reality, these three planes were Allied ones. With Phillips now believing that the element of surprise was lost, he decided to return to Singapore, much to the chagrin of his crews who had been on high alert for a surface engagement against the Japanese. Ironically, Japanese Admiral Kurita's surface force was only a few miles away to the north of Force Z. Coincident with all of this reconnaissance activity and the Japanese submarine's reporting of the British capital ships' presence, Japanese planes at Saigon quickly aborted their mission to attack Singapore and instead loaded torpedoes onto their land-based Mitsubishi G4M Betty and Mitsubishi G3M Nell bombers to begin the hunt for the British ships during the early evening hours. Due to rain and cloud cover, the Japanese bombers could not locate the British force and returned to their French Indochinese aerodromes, while Phillips steered Force Z to Singapore.

During his return voyage to Singapore, Admiral Phillips received some new intelligence that the Japanese were landing troops at Kuantan, which lies halfway down the eastern side of the Malayan Peninsula between Kota Bahru and Singapore Island. The British admiral immediately noted that the reported landings, if successful, would have the drastic effect of cutting the land supply line up the Malay Peninsula to the forces in the north. Phillips now elected to confront the Japanese landing there, but after arriving off Kuantan in the early dawn hours of 10 December, no enemy invasion force was sighted. Unbeknown to Phillips, his force had been stalked by the same Japanese submarine, *I-65*, since 0230 hours, with six torpedoes being fired at *Repulse*, all of which missed.

Japanese Admiral Nobutake Kondo, commander-in-chief of the Japanese invasion forces, had ordered all of his available naval aircraft to attack during the early morning hours of 10 December, while he sailed his surface vessels southwards to attack the British ships. In addition, the IJN launched against the British its twin-engine Nell and Betty bombers carrying both torpedoes and bombs southward again from their airfields in Indochina soon after dawn on 10 December. Phillips' whereabouts were unknown to the RAF or Singapore's command centre because he had kept radio silence. His decision to maintain radio silence was to hide his intentions to the enemy. However, by doing so, he had to rely on the Singapore command staff to anticipate his reaction to the Kuantan landing and automatically send fighters to cover his surface vessels. Phillips error then was to rely on the intelligence of his shore-based colleagues in following his line of reasoning, thus, the maintenance of radio silence and the absence of a clear request for Singapore-based fighter cover for Force *Z* off Kuantan. Another error involved those in Singapore, who were oblivious that their signal of the Kuantan landing, although false information, had been sent to Force *Z*, and it apparently never occurred to them that Phillips would head for that locale and rely on Singapore to send up the RAF and RAAF fighters for air cover.

At 1107 hours on 10 December, HMS *Repulse* and HMS *Prince of Wales* were attacked by ninety-six high-level horizontal and torpedo bombers as well as ten search planes sent out from Saigon before dawn. At 1113 hours, the high-level bombers scored one hit on the hangar deck area of HMS *Repulse*, which started a small fire. At 1140 hours, six torpedoes hit HMS *Prince of Wales*. Meanwhile, Captain Tennant of HMS *Repulse* had sent an emergency radio signal to Singapore at 1150 hours that Force *Z* was being attacked. This was the only signal ever received on shore to indicate that air support was urgently needed by HMS *Prince of Wales* and HMS *Repulse*. How Admiral Phillips believed that he would automatically be provided RAF or RAAF air cover if he ran into trouble while maintaining radio silence remains an enigma. Tennant, as well as print and radio correspondents, notably CBS correspondent Cecil Brown, aboard HMS *Repulse* were amazed at the tenacity of the Japanese torpedo pilots to press on with their near sea-level attacks despite withering British naval anti-aircraft fire. Nine torpedo bombers launched their torpedoes at the old battle cruiser. Six minutes after the solitary signal requesting air cover was sent, Tennant showed incredible skill of manoeuvre and succeeded in evading all the tracks of nine torpedoes. Just prior to sending the emergency radio signal to Singapore, Tennant had asked the flagship what damage she had suffered but got no answer. He then signalled Phillips, 'We have dodged nineteen torpedoes thus far, thanks to Providence,' adding that all damage done from the one Japanese bomb hit was under control.

Two minutes after the torpedo attack, HMS *Repulse* had some near misses from high-level bombers. Tennant now brought HMS *Repulse* closer to HMS *Prince of Wales* to ask if he could assist her. There was no reply. Soon it was HMS *Repulse*'s turn again to be attacked. A group of nine torpedo-bombers was spotted low on the horizon on the starboard bow. One torpedo struck home amidships 'with a great jarring shudder, as though a giant hand had shaken the ship', recalled one officer. Yet she still steamed at 25 knots with her 4-inch guns and eight-barrelled pom-poms attempting to provide anti-aircraft artillery cover for the wounded ship. HMS *Repulse* was hit by more torpedoes, as the planes were attacking from all directions so it was impossible for Captain Tennant to evade every track. Listing heavily, Captain Tennant ordered everyone on deck. Again he demonstrated decisive leadership and later reflected, 'the decision for a commanding officer to cease all work in the ship below, is an exceedingly difficult one, but knowing the ship's construction I felt very sure that she would not survive four torpedoes, and this was borne out, for she only remained afloat six or seven minutes after I gave the order for everyone to come on deck'. Captain Tennant recollected, when seeing 200 or 300 men collecting on the starboard side of the ship prior to its rolling over, 'I never saw the slightest sign of panic or ill discipline. I told them from the bridge how well they had fought the ship, and wished them good luck.' The escorting destroyers HMS *Electra* and HMS *Vampire* picked up the survivors, who numbered forty-two out of sixty-six officers (including Tennant) and 754 out of 1,240 ratings. At 1233 hours, HMS *Repulse* rolled over and plunged out of sight, stern first.

Barely able to make any speed, HMS *Prince of Wales*, having been hit by six torpedoes, was now under attack by nine high-level bombers. At 1244 hours, Japanese bombs were dropped with only one hitting the battleship. However, it caused the flagship to founder and when her beams were almost awash Captain Leach gave the order to abandon ship. At 1319 hours, HMS *Prince of Wales* keeled heavily to port and began to sink. As she went down, eleven Allied Brewster Buffalo fighters arrived on the scene, prompting a distant group of Japanese bombers to jettison their bombs and make for home. Tennant's emergency signal had reached the Air Operations Room at 1219 hours, and eleven RAAF Buffaloes of Squadron 453 were in the air only seven minutes later, having departed from Sembawang Airfield on the northern part of Singapore Island. Now the Buffaloes patrolled overhead while the survivors of both ships were picked out of the water or from floats and lifeboats. It has been reported that while swimming for their lives, the survivors of HMS *Repulse* gave three cheers for their captain and their lost ship. As for HMS *Prince of Wales*, both Captain Leach and Admiral Phillips went down with their ship, neither one making an attempt to save himself, while waving to their departing men. Leach, in fact, was heard to call out from the sinking vessel, 'Goodbye. Thank you. Good luck. God bless you.' HMS *Express*, an escorting destroyer, crammed ninety out of 110 officers and 1,195 out of 1,502 ratings aboard. Whether it was the presence of the Allied fighters or some other factor, the Japanese chose not to strafe the survivors in the water or the destroyers attempting to save the British seamen.

It is worth repeating that the Brewster Buffalo fighters were dispatched in response to the only message, that is Tennant's, for help that had come through from the task force. Also, Tennant had warned his crew twenty-four hours earlier to carry or wear their life-saving apparatus. When the squadron of Buffaloes, detailed to give air cover, arrived from Singapore, the sea was littered with wreckage and men floating around in the water waiting to be picked up by the destroyers. Curiously enough, the men were far from dispirited, as the pilot reported later: 'It was obvious that the three destroyers were going to take hours to pick up those hundreds of men clinging to bits of wreckage and swimming around in filthy, oily water. About all this the threat of another bombing and machine-gun attack was imminent. Every one of those men must have realized that. Yet as I flew round every man waved and put up his thumb as I flew over him. It shook me, for here was something above human nature.' According to Churchill's history of the Second World War, 'Captain Tennant realized that his ship was doomed. He promptly ordered all hands on deck, and there is no doubt that this timely action saved many lives.'

The cost to the Japanese for the sinking of two British capital ships was only eight aircraft. On the heels of the disaster at Pearl Harbor, the loss of Force *Z* brought grim prospects for the Allies at their isolated bastions in the Far East. All that was left for the RAF and RAAF in northern Malaya was to abandon their airfields, which had been the strategic linchpin all along for the defence of Singapore. Without an air presence in northern Malaya, British and Commonwealth troops would eventually be forced to retreat southwards towards Singapore barely ahead of the Japanese troops rapidly advancing down Malaya's western coast.

Admiral Sir Tom Phillips (*right*) with his chief of staff, Rear-Admiral Palliser, in Singapore before the ill-fated departure of Force *Z*. Fortunately Palliser remained in Singapore when Force *Z* sailed. (*NARA*)

An IJN Mitsubishi G3M2 (Nell) medium attack bomber in flight. Although relatively obsolete when the Malaya invasion began, this craft contributed greatly to the sinking of HMS *Prince of Wales* and HMS *Repulse*. Here the plane has bombs attached to its fuselage and was capable of delivering almost a ton of explosive. *(NARA)*

A formation of Mitsubishi G4M1 (Betty) medium attack bombers searching for Force *Z*. Initial searches for Force *Z* failed but the horizontal and torpedo bombers caught up with it on 10 December 1941 off Kuantan, Malaya. *(USAMHI)*

(*Above left*) Air crew of a Japanese Mitsubishi G4M1 (Betty) medium attack bomber search the South China Sea for Force Z's location. (*NARA*)

(*Above right*) Japanese naval air crew help to load bombs onto their twin-engined Mitsubishi G3M2 (Nell) medium attack bomber at an airfield in Indochina. (*NARA*)

Japanese naval pilots race to board their Mitsubishi G3M2 (Nell) medium attack bombers at their airfield near Saigon on 9 December 1941. (*USAMHI*)

A flight of IJN medium attack bombers sortie over the South China Sea in search of Force Z. The horizontal and sea-level torpedo bombers sank the HMS *Prince of Wales* and HMS *Repulse* within minutes of locating them, proving that a protective air cover was an absolute necessity even for capital ships. (*USAMHI*)

First Lord of the Admiralty, Winston S. Churchill (*left*) with his vice-chief of the naval staff, Admiral Sir Tom Phillips, in London in February 1940. The soon-to-be prime minister had great respect for Phillips' intellect, although some of his fellow admirals questioned his views on the invincibility of battleships to air attack as well as his own sea-going experience. (*NARA*)

HMS *Prince of Wales*, the flagship for Admiral Phillips Force Z entering Singapore Harbour. Churchill believed that Force Z's presence would be a deterrent to Japanese expansionist plans. (NARA)

HMS *Repulse* was a formidable battle cruiser for her day. However, the ship lacked sufficient horizontal armour for bomb protection and adequate anti-aircraft guns to repel aerial attack. Ironically it was Japanese torpedo planes flying at sea level that sunk her. (NARA)

One of HMS *Repulse's* hand-operated 4-inch anti-aircraft guns. This weapon had limited vertical positioning and was too few in numbers to mount an adequate aerial defence against a determined enemy, especially torpedo bombers at sea level. (*NARA*)

The Japanese *I-65* submarine, which was subsequently renamed *I-165* as shown in this photograph, initially spotted Force *Z* and unsuccessfully fired torpedoes at HMS *Repulse* the day before the IJN aerial assault. (*NARA*)

(*Opposite page*) An aerial view from an attacking Japanese plane on 10 December 1941. The HMS *Prince of Wales* (*top*) and the battle cruiser HMS *Repulse* early in the attack. *Repulse* has just sustained a bomb hit, evidenced by the plume of black smoke rising from the ship. Several near misses are also apparent on both sides of the vessel. (*NARA*)

Captain William G. Tennant, RN, who commanded the HMS *Repulse*. His brilliant naval career included co-ordinating the Royal Navy's evacuation of the BEF from the beaches and moles of Dunkirk in late May 1940. (*NARA*)

The crew of HMS *Prince of Wales* abandoning ship. The escorting destroyer HMS *Express* picks up survivors from the listing battleship. Moments after this photograph, the destroyer's lifelines had to be severed as HMS *Prince of Wales* was going to capsize imminently. These lucky survivors would arrive in Singapore only to become prisoners of the Japanese five weeks later. (*NARA*)

Captain Tenant (*left*) with Canon Bezzant, HMS *Repulse*'s ship chaplain, aboard the Australian destroyer *Vampire* after the rescue. (*NARA*)

Rescued survivors from HMS *Repulse* aboard the destroyer HMS *Electra*. Captain Tennant's early and decisive action to abandon ship contributed to the large percentage of HMS *Repulse*'s crew being saved. (*NARA*)

HMS *Prince of Wales* beginning to sink as seen from aboard one of the rescuing destroyers. *(NARA)*

RAAF Squadron flying Brewster Buffaloes with one Bristol Blenheim flying over Malaya. HMS *Repulse's* Captain Tennant sent an emergency signal to Singapore's Air Operations Room just over an hour after the aerial assault commenced. Immediately after, eleven RAAF Brewster Buffaloes of Squadron 453, such as those shown, were airborne and dispersed the Japanese bombers from further attack and strafing. *(AWM)*

Chapter Four

The British Response to the Malayan Invasion

Since the Japanese invasion of Manchuria in 1931, Whitehall was always wary of the possibility of an offensive against Malaya. Quite presciently in 1937, Major-General W.G.S. Dobbie, GOC Malaya, prepared an appreciation of a potential Japanese invasion. He stated that Japan would probably seize air bases in Thailand as well as conduct an amphibious assault at Singora and Patani in Thailand, along with eastern coastal sites such as Kota Bahru in Malaya. Despite such clairvoyance, Malaya's garrison was increased by only one battalion and monies for defence works were mostly allocated to machine-gun emplacements in Johore Province. Once war started with Germany in September 1939, the three service chiefs in Singapore formulated an appreciation for the chiefs-of-staff in London. Assuming that a British surface fleet would be wholly occupied with the German Navy, the principal defence for Malaya and Singapore would be air power. However, this potential defensive posture was almost immediately negated by a political understanding that Japanese entry into Thailand, along Malaya's northern frontier, would not be a cause for war between the two empires.

On 7 August 1941, Lieutenant-General Arthur E. Percival, who had assumed the role of GOC Malaya, informed the War Office of his need for six divisions of infantry for the defence of Malaya along with two regiments of tanks as well as ancillary anti-tank and anti-aircraft artillery units. As December 1941 loomed, the British Army in Malaya still was short two of its requested six infantry divisions as well as an absence of the requested armoured regiments and amplified anti-aircraft batteries. Further-more, rubber plantation owners did not want British and Commonwealth troops on their property. Thus, jungle training was minimal, the quality of troops patchy; and British Army officers fairly ignorant of jungle warfare, with the exception of, perhaps, the Argyll and Sutherland Highlanders as opposed to their Japanese counterparts, who were learning how to eventually manoeuvre through the dense Malayan jungle, largely through the efforts of Colonel Tsuji.

It turns out that the Japanese had not caught the British by surprise. At 0200 hours on 6 December 1941, RAAF airmen, flying a Lockheed Hudson bomber based at

Kota Bahru, alerted ACM Sir Robert Brooke-Popham, C-in-C Far East, at his general headquarters, about Japanese convoys heading for Thailand's east coast. It was up to Brooke-Popham, still C-in-C until General Sir Henry Pownall's arrival in late December to replace him, to decide whether to order implementation of Operation *Matador* or to position his troops along a fixed line of defences at Jitra, a small village at a road junction in northern Kedah Province 18 miles south of the Thai frontier. Operation *Matador* was to dispatch Major General David Murray-Lyon's 11th Indian Division from its incomplete defensive base at Jitra, by road and rail, to the eastern Thai coastal site at Singora, 130 miles away. On 5 December, Brooke-Popham was given permission to implement Operation *Matador* without conferring with the War Office if he had positive information of the Japanese sailing with the intent of landing on the Kra Isthmus or violating any other part of Thailand. Upon hearing about the Japanese fleet sailing for Thailand, the British Army GOC in Malaya, Lieutenant-General Percival, had duly ordered his 11th Indian Division at Jitra to move north and stand-by to defend possible landing areas according to the pre-arranged Operation *Matador* plan. Murray-Lyon's troops were enthusiastic about smashing the Japanese invasion forces. However, the British C-in-C Far East then dithered. As no state of war existed, Brooke-Popham was not going to start one by setting Operation *Matador* into motion by himself. Parenthetically, this was also the posture that both the Foreign Office and Churchill wanted to take. Thus, if hostilities broke out in Southeast Asia, it would not be due to a pre-emptive British offensive move. In any event, Operation *Matador* was never executed in response to the sighting of the Japanese invasion fleet on 6 December 1941.

After hostilities commenced, the British strategy was always defensive and lacked any tactical brilliance. At 0800 hours on 8 December, staff officers at Percival's headquarters in Singapore phoned Brooke-Popham for permission to still put Operation *Matador* into effect. Brooke-Popham squandered two hours and, in that time, decided to cancel the operation for quasi-political reasons. He also offered as an excuse that the Japanese landings were too strong to oppose. In fact, Percival was also dithering about ordering Operation *Matador* to commence. He was of the opinion that an encounter between the Japanese landing force and his 11th Indian Division contingents would be a risky endeavour, especially if the Japanese landed tanks as the British had none. So, Percival informed Brooke-Popham that he now considered Operation *Matador* unsound and the latter ordered the Indian troops to return to Jitra's defence. Further hours were wasted until Percival could be located and then transmit the order for Murray-Lyon's division to fall-back. After the decision not to execute Operation *Matador*, Percival sent the 11th Indian Division to Jitra to defend the airfield nearby and preserve the vital link to both Thailand and, consequently, Burma. However, due to the planning for Operation *Matador*, this division had done little preparatory work on their defensive line until the evening of 10 December.

On 8 December, the IJA 5th Division, under the command of Lieutenant-General Matsui, landed without any local resistance at Singora and Patani in Thailand and was now prepared to head south-west into the Kedah Province of north-western Malaya. This division was comprised of recruits from the Hiroshima district and consisted of many veterans from campaigning in China, where it had served continuously from 1937 to 1941, becoming renowned for its atrocities committed against the Chinese citizenry. Also, the Japanese 3rd Air Division quickly established itself at Singora and began aerial assault all along northern Malaya. Due chiefly to ineffective RAF fighter defence, along with inadequate anti-aircraft artillery fire, the 3rd Air Division wreaked havoc among British planes still on the ground in north-western Malaya, because of faulty warning systems, as well as local Malay villages, the latter of which helped to spread terror among the civilian population, be they European or Asian. By the evening of 8 December, RAF strength was reduced in northern Malaya from 110 planes to fifty and the Japanese were to possess complete air superiority for the rest of the campaign.

The Chrysanthemum (18th IJA) Division's Takumi Force (56th Infantry Regiment) loaded into assault craft shortly before midnight on 7 December. These troops were recruited from the Kurume district and had been in China since 1937. Thought to be one of the finest IJA divisions, under the command of Lieutenant-General Renya Mutaguchi, these troops had campaigned with the 5th Division in China and were stationed from February 1940 to August 1941 in Indochina. Due to rough seas, it was not until 0100 hours on 8 December that Colonel Nasu's 56th Infantry Regiment headed for Kota Bahru, where they initially met heavy resistance. At 0130 hours, Nasu signalled Takumi, 'succeeded in landing but there are many obstacles. Send second wave.' At 0200 hours, RAF aircraft bombed the convoy scoring a hit on Takumi's HQ ship, the *Awajisan Maru*, leading the naval escort commander to suggest calling off the landing and heading out to sea away from the threat of aerial assault. Takumi refused and continued the second wave's landing despite the need to abandon the *Awajisan Maru* and the heavy Japanese casualties that were being incurred from wired-in British and Commonwealth machine-gun positions. Takumi later wrote, 'there was utmost confusion on the beach, but the commander realized that if they remained where they were, they would be killed to a man, so the order was "go on".' Eventually, the Japanese assault troops began to circumvent the British and Commonwealth positions and were able to get behind them for rifle, grenade and flamethrower attack.

Kota Bahru was defended by the 8th Indian Infantry Brigade but by mid-afternoon their central positions had been taken. The RAF airfield at Kota Bahru was bombed and strafed with much damage to aircraft and installations. At 1900 hours, Brigadier Key received permission to withdraw his troops although elements of the Takumi

Force had suffered 15 per cent casualties. Therefore, the 18th IJA Division reaped success by capturing Kota Bahru by tenaciously attacking despite initial setbacks.

Yamashita's Imperial Guards Division was to capture Bangkok and then move south to join the rest of the 25th Army in Malaya at a later date. This division was recruited from all districts in Japan in order to fulfil the highest physical standards, principally height, in order to protect the emperor as its primary responsibility. In June 1941, this three-regiment field division was formed around the nucleus of the 2nd Guards Brigade and trained especially for the Malayan campaign on Hainan Island before being transferred to southern Indochina in July 1941 with the permission of the Vichy Government in France. Yamashita's infantry was reinforced by an armoured division of more than 230 light and medium tanks. As for air power, Yamashita commanded the 3rd Air Division of 354 first-line aircraft based in Indochina as well as being supported by the IJN's 22nd Air Flotilla, with its 180 aircraft, stationed in Saigon.

Major-General David Murray-Lyon, a Scot whose 11th Indian Division defended north-western Malaya, was prepared to initiate Operation *Matador*. However, with the vacillations of Percival and Brooke-Popham, this division instead fought the monsoon by repairing water-logged trench systems and hastily wiring in machine-gun defensive emplacements and laying anti-tank mines. Because the 11th Indian Division had wasted so much time awaiting Brooke-Popham's decision on Operation *Matador*, the Jitra line of defences looked like a rundown construction site. Murray-Lyon had known that his chances of holding the incomplete defences and poor terrain constituting the Jitra line were slim. In order to give the Indian 6th and 15th Brigades the necessary preparatory time for erecting defences at Jitra, Murray-Lyon sent the 1/14th Punjabis of the 15th Brigade north to Changlun to delay the Japanese advance. This chaotic, piecemeal attempt to counter the Japanese assault demonstrated the weakness revealed on multiple occasions by the British commanders in Malaya to follow-up with drawn-up plans. After a heavy bombing raid on the Alor Star airfield on 9 December, the RAF chose to abandon it. Thus, the 11th Indian Division was going to fight at Jitra to protect Alor Star, the capital of Kedah Province, to enable the RAF to maintain their presence at the airfield, which was in the process of being abandoned.

The Japanese were always advancing, thereby making Percival's plans to counter appear sluggish. After Yamashita had secured Kota Bahru, because its airfield threatened his landings just across the border in Thailand, he knew that the way to invade Malaya was down the western coast which, unlike the underdeveloped eastern side of the peninsula, had good north-south roads all the way to Singapore. The next vital position for the Japanese to drive the British and Commonwealth forces from was at Jitra, which lies in the Malayan province of Kedah Province, located south of Sadao in Thailand in north-western Malaya on the Singora-Alor Star main trunk road. The presence of airfields at Alor Star, 12 miles to the south of Jitra, made this location a position of vital importance to both sides. There were other Allied airfields to the south of Jitra at Sungei Patani and Butterworth. At Jitra, the west coast railway and road trunk came together and ran parallel with one another for 50 miles until they separated on to Butterworth and the ferry point for Penang Island. The IJA 5th Division was ordered to move west on Jitra from Singora and Patani on the eastern coast of Thailand.

Major-General Murray-Lyon's task was daunting as he had to defend too much frontage in north-western Malaya with his 15th, 6th and 28th Brigades. Neither brigade could support the other while support within units of each brigade was limited. Mixed in with the brigades of the 11th Indian Division were the three regular British Army battalions from the Argyll and Sutherland Highlanders, the East Surreys and the Leicesters. They totalled over 2,000 men and comprised a fifth of the division's infantry, being considered the most ready and jungle-trained. When the British generals before the war wanted local labour to improve the Jitra defences, they were told that the rubber plantations and tin mines had priority. When a plan was offered to secure the British left flank to the sea by flooding an area of a rice paddy, that too was rejected as food supplies in Malaya could not be compromised in the name of amplifying a defensive position. The troops ultimately allocated the job of defending Jitra were the 1/14th Punjabi of 15th Brigade and by the evening of 10 December they were occupying a position at Changlun.

At 0800 hours on 11 December, this unit was attacked by Lieutenant-Colonel Saeki's Reconnaissance Unit support by ten light and medium tanks. After some of the Punjabi positions had become compromised, Brigadier Garrett withdrew the battalion to an intermediate position just to the north of Jitra and gave them the task of holding it overnight. However, while the men were moving their anti-tank guns and equipment in steady rain, Saeki attacked with tanks and infantry in trucks, catching the rear of the column and wreaking havoc upon it as it was sheltering under the rubber trees from the teeming rain. After the destruction of the Punjabis, the Japanese attacked the 2/1st Gurkhas and a battalion of the 28th Brigade.

Saeki launched an attack on the 2/9th Jats at 2030 hrs on 11 December. However, stiff artillery and machine-gunfire broke the assault. Saeki made another assault against the British centre, but they held out until a Japanese flanking attack panicked the remnants of the 11th Indian Division. Murray-Lyon asked his III Corps commander, General Heath, permission to withdraw to a more suitable anti-tank barrier and, after some vacillation, at 2200 hours he received orders that the his division would withdraw from Jitra 15 miles to the south. By the afternoon of 11 December, the 5th IJA Division was engaging the lead elements of the 11th Indian Division. Although the initial assault by the two lead battalions of the 5th IJA Division was being repulsed by the Indian right flank, the British division commander, fearing an encirclement that would cut him off to his east, ordered a withdrawal. In characteristic fashion, the

Japanese infantry exploited the hasty retreat by the 11th Indian Division and forced the evacuation of Penang Island on 16 December and the abandonment of numerous barges, motor launches and junks that would be used later by the IJA for flanking attacks by sea.

The British retreat was disorderly with the Japanese in pursuit of the divisional rearguard and at 0430 hours on 12 December, the engagement temporarily ceased. The debacle at Jitra for the British was disastrous with British casualties running into the thousands coupled with the loss of guns, vehicles, supplies, ammunition and, more importantly, morale. Japanese casualties were under fifty men and their morale soared, in addition to the captured weaponry, ammunition, vehicles, fuel and food stocks. Most importantly, the British lost the initiative after Jitra as there would not now be time to adequately establish and man defensive positions in Johore Province and Singapore. As the retreat continued southerly after the loss at Jitra, British morale sunk to even lower depths. The Japanese advance, in large part, was due to Colonel Tsuji's inclusion of engineer regiments to repair damaged bridges, and in this way deprive the element of time for the British to establish new defensive positions. Now that all Allied opposition was crushed in north-west Malaya, Yamashita ordered his Takumi Detachment to deal with the 9th Indian Division on the east coast after landing reinforcements at Kota Bahru. Yamashita's goal was to occupy Kuala Lumpur, the Federated States capital, by mid-January, in order to reach the Straits of Johore by 31 January. A large part of Yamashita's success in north-western Malaya's Kedah Province was the use of the tank by the Japanese to spearhead their infantry. The main tank was the Type 97 Chi-Ha medium tank, which had a 57mm gun and two machine-guns. The tank could run at a speed of 24 miles per hour for 130 miles. The British had no tanks and could only answer with their 2-pounder anti-tank guns if they were unlimbered and in ambush position concealed from the Japanese.

During the subsequent days after the British defeat at Jitra, battles occurred on 14–15 December at Gurun, a road junction astride the railway where rice paddies from the western plains merge into south Kedah's rubber plantations, about 30 miles to the south of Jitra on western Malaya's coast. Remnants of Murray-Lyon's 11th Indian Division received reinforcements (12th and 6th Brigades) from Percival after he withdrew his battered troops, first to behind the Krian River and then on the line of the Perak River.

On 16 December, Penang Island was evacuated on the west coast of Malaya. Penang Island, with its harbour located at Georgetown, had been viewed as a fortress since 1936 by the British. It was another vital site that Yamashita's 25th Army had to seize to keep his coastal flank free of any Allied air or seaborne attack as he descended the western side of the Malay Peninsula in his drive towards Singapore. Another reason for the British desire to retain Penang Island was its underwater communication cables with both Ceylon and India and, therefore, London and the

War Cabinet. Percival had a contingency plan to defend Penang Island but, like many of his others, it fell apart when the 11th Indian Division, which was to add support to the island's garrison, was routed at Jitra and now in full retreat. Also, the island's garrison had been ferried over to the mainland in an attempt to halt the Japanese advance, so in essence, there were no first-rate troops to defend Penang Island. After daily bombings since 8 December, the island's defences, which did not include any anti-aircraft guns, and the civilian population were severely damaged and injured respectively. Over 2,000 civilians were killed on 11 December in a particularly heavy raid on the population centre of Georgetown. There was a meaningful RAAF fighter response with Brewster Buffalo aircraft sortied from Singapore to Butterworth immediately opposite the island, with some downing of Japanese bombers on 13 and 14 December. By 15 December, the aerial assault on the island stopped. However, the harm to the civilian population's morale and the island's infrastructure had been overwhelming. On 12 December, the island's commander and civil authority both ordered the evacuation of all Europeans, although the population of Penang Island was predominantly Asian. The first evacuations of the Europeans from Penang Island began on the night of 13–14 December.

However, nothing seemed to be able to stop the Japanese juggernaut as they crossed sequential east-to-west running rivers with only minimal opposition as they pursued the 11th Indian Division throughout Kedah Province. On 13 December, the Japanese attacked down the main western road trunk with tanks and trucks loaded with infantry. On 15 December, the III Corps commander, General Heath, after having arrived in Kedah Province two days earlier from Kuala Lumpur to assess the situation, ordered the evacuation of the small Penang garrison with several hundred European men for the night of 16–17 December as the Asians were left behind. On the morning of 16 December, the retreating 11th Indian Division was already south of the Muda River and had passed into Province Wellesley, on Malaya's west coast, in which Butterworth was situated, with the intent of moving further south into Perak Province. Two companies from the Japanese 5th Division arrived unopposed in Georgetown at 1600 hours on 19 December. Yamashita had captured Penang Island without firing a shot. It was Yamashita's assessment that the British were demoralized and would fight only sporadically behind the barriers that the rivers posed to the Japanese advance. Even so, III Corps Commander Heath, on 20 December, decided to let the Japanese cross the Perak River without any opposition from the 11th Indian Division, enabling this battered formation to make a stand further south, but in the process conceding much more territory in the process.

The capture of Kota Bahru on 8 December was followed by a continued steady southwards advance down the eastern coast of the Malay Peninsula, ultimately forcing the 9th Indian Division into Kuantan, halfway between Kota Bahru and Singapore, by the end of December. On 23 December, General Sir Henry Pownall arrived in Singapore to relieve Air Chief Marshal Sir Robert Brooke-Popham as C-in-C Far East, and was to assume control on 27 December. Contemporaneous with Pownall's appointment, Percival, as GOC Malaya, countered by allowing the 9th Indian Division to extract itself west of Kuantan in order to defend Kuala Lumpur, the capital of the Malay States. However, in order to achieve this, the 11th Indian Division needed to occupy defensive positions in Kampar on 27 December. The 5th IJA Division attacked Kampar on 30 December, but the 11th Indian Division held out against the usual Japanese infantry tactics of flank attacks and infiltration. The Japanese response was to launch an amphibious westward turning movement, using the watercraft captured at Penang Island and the small boats brought overland from the Singora landing. Again, the 11th Indian Division, without sufficient reserves to repel the Japanese landings, had to withdraw again under the constant threat of aerial bombardment and strafing. By 2 January 1942, Percival pulled the remnants of the 11th Division to behind the Slim River. Pownall, who knew Percival from the BEF in France in 1940, wrote in his diary, he is 'an uninspiring leader and rather gloomy. I hope it won't mean that I have to relieve Percival […] But it might so happen.' Technically, in fact, as of 30 December 1941, when Churchill appointed Wavell, then C-in-C India, Supreme Commander South West Pacific (the ABDA command), Pownall after only three days in his post as C-in-C Far East stepped down and prepared to become Wavell's chief of staff. Brooke-Popham had been relieved earlier as C-in-C Far East by Churchill himself.

On 7 January 1942, on his visit to Singapore to inspect the defences on the north side of the fortress island, Wavell found nothing erected nor any detailed plans made for resistance against a land invasion from across the Straits of Johore. The field marshal had also learned that almost all of the island's great guns, the Buono Vista and Johore batteries were facing either the sea or the Johore River to the east of Singapore Island, and could not be turned to fire at the advancing Japanese coming southwards down the Malay Peninsula. Only the 6- and 9.2-inch guns on Blankang Mati Island, to the south of Keppel Harbour on Singapore Island's southern shore, could be turned to fire inland. However, these batteries were equipped with mostly armour-piercing shells for ships. Percival's chief engineer, Ivan Simson, at this time also badgered the Malayan Army commander that not only was there a need to erect fixed defences in Johore for the exhausted 11th Indian Division to retreat into and fight behind them but also an absence and shortage of time to secure the northern and north-western shores of Singapore should an evacuation of the peninsula to Singapore Island become necessary while the southern shore of the island bristled with defences. Percival gave the lame excuse that erecting fixed northern shore defences would weaken civilian morale while those in Johore would rob the 11th Indian Division of an offensive fighting spirit. A few days after his encounters with

Wavell and Simson, Percival directed his engineers to prepare a series of obstacles, mainly anti-tank ones, on the northern shore.

The supercilious British commanders on Malaya and Singapore Island could not have foreseen such a rapid advance by Yamashita's three divisions, comprising his 25th Army. In fact, a captured British officer from the Royal Engineers had told Colonel Masanobu Tsuji that he had expected the defences in northern Malaya to hold out for substantially longer than the few weeks that they had. He mentioned, 'As the Japanese Army had not beaten the weak Chinese Army after four years' fighting in China we did not consider it a very formidable enemy.'

The month of January brought further disasters for the British and Commonwealth troops defending the Malay States to the north, although the Japanese 5th Division was delayed for a few days by the floodwaters of the Perak River. Then, being unopposed, the Japanese crossed the Perak River and advanced in strength down the motor road trunk towards the Slim River, which flows east-to-west near Telok Anson. After some fighting in Telok Anson, in which the Japanese 4th Guards Regiment and the 5th Division's 11th Infantry Regiment were amphibiously landed on 1 January 1942, British troops disengaged to the natural shelter of the Slim River. However, on 5 January, the Japanese were making landings at Selangor and Port Swettenham, which were 70 miles behind the 11th Division in southern Perak Province. On the eastern coast, the Allied 9th Division was retreating into central Malaya from Kuantan. The III Corps commander, General Heath, was forced to abandon the airfield at Kuantan. Percival was already of the mindset that eventually III Corps would have to execute a retreat in stages into northern Johore, where the final stand on the mainland would be made, which meant that Kuala Lumpur would also eventually be abandoned.

The Japanese began their attack on the Slim River line on 5 January and were initially beaten off by two Indian battalions of the 12th Indian Brigade, resulting in heavy enemy casualties. However, on the night of 7 January, Japanese tanks attacked down the motor trunk road and cleared the Indian road-blocks before any Allied anti-tank guns could be employed, resulting in the retreat of the Indian 12th Brigade pell mell. The attack across the Slim River continued a few miles to the south where the Japanese engaged the 28th Indian Brigade. Allied units comprised of Gurkhas and Punjabis were badly mauled and the Japanese were soon to control the Slim River road-bridge with all of the 11th Indian Division's motor transport trapped on the far side. Casualties among the 12th and 28th Indian Brigades approached 80 per cent. After the Japanese captured all of the division's artillery, including sixteen 25-pounder guns and seven 2-pounder anti-tank guns as well as motor transport, only about 1,000 British and Indian soldiers from the 11th Indian Division were able to make their escape south by foot. The retreating British and Commonwealth forces were under orders to destroy all resources that could be used by the enemy. According to the Official British History of the war in the Far East, 'The action at the Slim River was a major disaster. It resulted in the early abandonment of Central Malaya and gravely prejudiced reinforcing formations, then on their way to Singapore, to arm and prepare for battle [...] The immediate causes of the disaster were the failure to make full use of the anti-tank weapons available.' Brigadier General Ian Stewart of the 12th Brigade accepted his share of the blame both in the choice of a brigade head-quarters, which put him out of contact with his troops, and for not deploying the field artillery in an anti-tank role. Stewart confessed that he had no prior experience combating tanks at night or in using field artillery in an anti-tank role, which was common practice among the British formations fighting Rommel along the North African littoral. In addition, the motor road bridge across the Slim River was not demolished by the British, thereby enabling the Japanese advance to continue unimpeded. Major General Archie Paris, who had replaced Murray-Lyon as com-mander of the 11th Indian Division and had initially added some esprit to that demoralized fighting unit after Jitra, was demoted by III Corps Commander Heath. Paris returned to his former command of the 12th Brigade, while Brigadier Stewart rejoined the Argyll and Sutherland Highlanders as their commander.

To compound the operational dysfunction at GOC, Malaya headquarters, Wavell arrived on 7 January 1942 and accepted the Australian General Gordon Bennett's, and not Percival's, plans for the defence of Johore. General Sir Henry Pownall noted in his diary that Wavell was 'not at all happy about Percival, who has the knowledge, but not the personality to carry through a tough fight'. Clearly, Percival had lost Wavell's vote of approval for his command style. After the crossing of the Slim River, Wavell drove north to find III Corps disorganized and the 11th Indian Division completely shattered. Wavell too recognized that the disaster at the Slim River necessitated the shifting of the entire British line back to the southern tip of the Malay Peninsula, and so ordered a general withdrawal of the Indian troops of almost 150 miles south-east to Johore Province for re-organization. There would now be nothing between the victorious Japanese and Kuala Lumpur. A new line was formed with the 9th Indian and the rested 8th Australian Divisions, the latter of which was already positioned in Johore, to hold along the Muar River on the western coast, while the remnants of III Corps defended the eastern coast at Mersing. Major-General Gordon Bennett's Australians would be entrusted, in large part, to make the final attempt to stop Yamashita's Japanese onslaught, while the battle-weary 9th Division would contribute to the line's defence. The remnants of the 11th Indian Division would refit in Johore as it was unfit for combat in its present state.

Despite the visit by Wavell on 7–8 January to both Singapore and forward areas on the peninsula and an expectation that the soon-to-arrive British 18th Division, com-prising fresh Territorial units from East Anglia, would reinforce the Australians giving Bennett some offensive punch, Yamashita committed troops of the Guards Division, which reached Ipoh and was bringing more of Mutaguchi's 18th IJA Division down to Johore by road. Wavell had ascertained first-hand during his visit to the forward areas on the peninsula on 8 January that the 9th and 11th Indian Divisions 'with very few exceptions are no longer fit to withstand attack'. Wavell, on 9 January, discussed his plan with Bennett at Johore Bahru, that a decisive battle should be fought on the north-west frontier of Johore near the mouth of the Muar River using the Australian 8th Division (less the 22nd Brigade), that had been stationed in Mersing, and the 45th Indian Brigade as the main Allied force. The 9th Indian Division and the 45th Indian Brigade would come under Bennett's command (Westforce) while Heath's III Corps would withdraw into southern Johore Province defending a line running from Mersing on the east coast through Kluang in central Johore to the town of Batu Pahat on the west coast to essentially rest and re-fit. The Australian 22nd Brigade would remain in Mersing but re-join the Australian 8th Division on the Muar after it could be relieved by reinforcements from Singapore Island. Then, Wavell met Percival and presented the plan devised with Bennett as a done deal, which was the direct opposite of Percival's plan that the Australians would defend the east coast of Johore Province while Heath's III Corps held the west coast. Wavell and Bennett's plan depended on holding the Japanese in northern Johore Province until reinforcements could be mustered on Singapore Island, which would not be before the middle of February, for an Allied counter-attack against Yamashita's forces on the peninsula. Already the 5th IJA Division had entered Kuala Lumpur on 11 January, the main base of British III Corps, capturing copious amounts of supplies and equipment there.

Initially, Bennett's fresh Australian troops gained some success against the Japanese, principally by ambushing them on the Muar-Bakri road west of Gemas on 14–15 January. However, the Japanese were to cross the Muar River without much opposition as Bennett believed that the bulk of Japanese forces would attack down the trunk road in the vicinity of Gemas. At the Muar River, the 4th Japanese Guards Regiment annihilated the Indian companies of the Rajputana Rifles, which had been poorly positioned on the north side of a river that did not have a bridge to retreat over. At 0200 hours on 16 January, the Japanese crossed the river in force a few miles upstream of the Indians and established a road-block. Yamashita had just turned Bennett's left flank and when the 45th Indian Brigade began its withdrawal, Westforce was in danger of becoming surrounded. Wavell, having left Singapore for Java on 10 January, had always regretted that he did not send the Australian 22nd Brigade to Bennett to stiffen up Westforce prior to being replaced at Mersing by reinforcements. It was clear that even Bennett's Australians could not stem the Japanese tide as it methodically kept demolishing each new static line of defence that the Commonwealth forces established, even though they were inflicting casualties on the Japanese. On the afternoon of 18 January, the British now knew that the entire Imperial Guards Division was in the Muar area while the Japanese 5th Division was on the main road heading south. Despite a trickle of reinforcements from Singapore that Percival had dispatched to the peninsula, Bennett knew that unless the Westforce retreated, his main force would be destroyed. So Bennett's command was forced to withdraw from north-west Johore Province, which was effected on the evening of 19 January, over the one narrow bridge spanning a deep gorge of the Segamat River. In fact, the depleted 45th Indian Brigade had held up the Imperial Guards long enough to save Westforce from encirclement. After the Battle of the Muar, 45th Indian Brigade ceased to exist.

On 19 January, Wavell learned that there was no formalized plan to withdraw to Singapore Island. Wavell cabled Percival, 'You must think out the problem of how to withdraw from the mainland […] and how to prolong resistance on the island.' Percival, in response to Wavell's cables, planned for his Malayan forces to retreat in three columns and for the establishment of a bridge-head covering the passage through Johore Bahru. The following day, 20 January, Wavell met with Percival on Singapore to plan for the island's defence since the battle on the mainland appeared to be already a foregone conclusion to the field marshal. To his disliking, Wavell found that very little had been done to strengthen the island's northern defences and outlined some of his thoughts to augment defensive capabilities. Even Churchill entered the fray on 20 January and signalled Wavell, 'I want to make it absolutely clear that I expect every inch of ground to be defended, every scrap of material for defences to be blown to pieces to prevent capture by the enemy, and no question of surrender to be entertained until after protracted fighting among the ruins of Singapore City.' On 21 January, Wavell replied to Churchill that he had little hope of a drawn-out defence of Singapore Island as the prime minister had envisioned once the battle for Johore was lost. Wavell reiterated the obvious, namely that the fortress guns were sited for use against ships, and most of the ammunition was armour-piercing rather than high-explosive or anti-personnel.

The Japanese were not idle and launched three divisions in southern Johore against the British line there, necessitating Percival on 24 January to issue orders for the withdrawal from the southern Malay Peninsula to the island should it become necessary. On 28 January, Percival informed his divisional commanders that the evacuation should be carried out on the night of 30–31 January to form another defensive line on the island across the 2–3km-wide Straits of Johore. By dawn of 31 January, the entire British forces were over and preparations went forward to destroy the causeway across the Straits of Johore. Just after dawn, a skirl of bagpipes was heard as the shattered remnants, all ninety of them, of the Argyll and Sutherland Highlanders were the last men to leave the Malayan Peninsula. At 0800 hours, the causeway was blown up. Those who saw the separation of the island from the peninsula harboured some re-assurance about their distance from the Japanese across Singapore Island's moat. However, they were also clearly unaware that the Straits of Johore were scarcely 4 feet deep at low tide where the causeway once stood.

Malayan native pulls in soldiers of the Dogra Regiment on exercises in assorted craft on a lake near Singapore City in November 1941.
(*Library of Congress*)

Australian soldiers with their personal weapons in portable two-man rubber assault boats row across a Malayan waterway before the outbreak of war.
(*Library of Congress*)

A British Bren carrier on a Malayan road during pre-invasion training. Few British or Commonwealth units were adept at jungle field craft and with their vehicles had the unfortunate tendency to become road-bound, enabling the Japanese to outflank them all too often. (*USAMHI*)

British troops ride in an armoured troop carrier while on drills in Malaya. The reliance on mechanical transport became a liability for the British and Commonwealth forces in Malayan terrain, which the general staff believed was unsuitable for tanks. (*USAMHI*)

The 2nd Battalion of the Argyll and Sutherland Highlanders did prepare for fighting off-road. Here, two Highlanders deploy from a Lanchester armoured car with the soldier in the foreground carrying a machine-gun with a bipod in a rubber plantation. (*USAMHI*)

Japanese troops march single file through a rocky Malayan waterway surrounded by dense jungle. These soldiers had learned much of their jungle field craft from Colonel Tsuji's Taiwan Army No. 82 Unit, which in 1941 was charged with learning and preparing for fighting in Pacific war regions such as Malaya, Indonesia, the Philippine Islands and Burma. (*USAMHI*)

Heavily laden Japanese troops march across yet another Malayan waterway surrounded by jungle. Colonel Tsuji knew that newer methods for fighting in jungle terrain were needed for an army that had been fighting in China for the past decade. *(USAMHI)*

A Chinese man in north-western Malaya tries to repair some of his bombed hut after the Japanese aerial assaults began in Kedah Province on 8 December 1941.
(*Library of Congress*)

Malay soldiers look at debris in a north-western Malayan village after a Japanese air attack soon after hostilities commenced. (*USAMHI*)

Australian troops dig their foxholes in a rubber plantation. A machine-gun has been set-up in the background. Many of the Malayan rubber estate owners objected to the use of their property by the military being a source of continual friction up until the opening of hostilities. (AWM)

Two British 3-inch mortar crews set up their pieces and prepare to fire on Japanese positions in Malaya soon after the invasion. (USAMHI)

A Japanese Type 92 tank helps support the infantry during an assault through a Malayan village. General Yamashita had the distinct advantage using armour since the Allies had only mortars and 2-pounder anti-tank guns to stop them. The 25-pounder field artillery pieces were not effectively put to use as anti-tank weapons as they had been in North Africa. (USAMHI)

A Japanese Type 95 light tank with its 37mm gun traversed moves through dense Malayan vegetation on the periphery of a village to assist in an infantry assault. (USAMHI)

A British machine-gun emplacement in a concrete pillbox is assaulted by a Japanese soldier who is about to hurl in hand grenades to neutralize it during the battle of Jitra in Kedah Province in early December 1941. (USAMHI)

A Japanese infantry section advances almost doubled over beside a railroad track in an attempt to outflank their Allied opponents on the western side of the Malayan Peninsula. The officers lying prone in the foreground are trying to spot Allied firing positions with their binoculars. (USAMHI)

Stretcher bearers on Singapore Island aid a wounded soldier from the Malayan Peninsula onto an ambulance early in the conflict. (*USAMHI*)

An Allied soldier with his hands up looks bewildered as he surrenders to the invading Japanese. The helmeted Japanese solider (*left*) holding onto the prisoner is an officer, as he carries a long sword and a binoculars case. The helmeted Japanese soldier to the right of the prisoner holds his Mk. I helmet of First World War vintage. (*AWM*)

Commonwealth troops disembark from an uncovered lorry during the retreat down the Malayan Peninsula. (*AWM*)

Medical personnel attend a wounded British soldier on the Malayan Peninsula early in the conflict. Note the motorcycle that one of the medical officers utilized leaning against the tree. (*USAMHI*)

British sappers use a hydraulic drill in order to prepare a bridge for demolition during the retreat in early 1942.
(*Library of Congress*)

British sappers inserting their demolition charges into a bridge's infrastructure as Malay natives casually cross the bridge with their bicycles.
(*USAMHI*)

(*Above*) Japanese soldiers cross over a makeshift wooden plank bridge over a Malayan waterway besides the concrete support of a destroyed steel girder road bridge. Note that many of the Japanese infantry have their bicycles with them for the crossing. (*USAMHI*)

(*Opposite above*) Heavily camouflaged Japanese Type 97 *Chi-Ha* medium tank with its 57mm turret gun in traversed position. (*USAMHI*)

(*Opposite below*) Malay troops, some shirtless, attacking a Japanese position in a Malayan town. They carry the typical assortment of Allied weapons including a Bren light-machine-gun, a Sten light-machine-gun, and the SMLE rifle. (*USAMHI*)

(*Above*) Georgetown, the capital of Penang Island, as it appeared before the invasion. The general staff in Singapore erroneously labelled this a fortress as it was captured without firing a shot at the Japanese who crossed over from the Peninsula on their advance down the western side. (*NARA*)

(*Opposite page*) A European mother shows her happiness as she and her child, having been evacuated from Penang Island, arrive at the train station at Ipoh rail station in Perak Province. (*Library of Congress*)

(*Below*) A photograph of Georgetown before the war with many signs in Chinese, foreboding how many Asians were to be left behind in the evacuation to the Malayan Peninsula, while Europeans were given preference in Penang Island's abandonment. (*NARA*)

European evacuees from Penang
Island arrive at Ipoh rail station and
get refreshment from the local
residents there in Perak Province.
(*Library of Congress*)

A warning sign about a minefield that
had been set up by British sappers in
their retreat down the Malay
Peninsula. (*USAMHI*)

Japanese infantry stand beside their light tank in their advance through Kuala Lumpur, the capital of the Federated Malay States. *(USAMHI)*

Street fighting in Kuala Lumpur as two infantrymen cautiously advance in the open while two others provide covering fire. *(USAMHI)*

(*Above*) Four Japanese infantrymen racing through a Kuala Lumpur street as smoke from fires billows in the background. (*USAMHI*)

(*Opposite above*) Japanese troops advancing through a street in Kuala Lumpur. The infantryman lying on his side has a grenade launcher, which was often misnamed by the Allies as a knee mortar. (*USAMHI*)

(*Opposite below*) Japanese infantry advance on the Kuala Lumpur railway yards, which are ablaze. The Commonwealth rear guard was under orders to burn anything that might be of value to the invading Japanese forces. (*USAMHI*)

A sword-wielding Japanese officer leads infantry through a destroyed Kuala Lumpur street as bicycles lie discarded on the side of the road. (USAMHI)

Japanese sentries guard huts full of captured petrol, which helped propel the Japanese forces down the Malayan Peninsula. General Yamashita instructed his subordinates to press the attack and not wait for re-supply in anticipation of capturing enemy stores. (USAMHI)

British and Commonwealth forces burn rubber supplies in Malaya as a large black plume of smoke rises into the air. (*Library of Congress*)

The 8th Australian Division headquarters under camouflage in Johore Province. Field Marshal Wavell and General Bennett devised a plan for the defence of Johore Province, which directly contradicted that of General Percival. (*AWM*)

An Australian Bren light-machine-gun crew takes a cigarette break in Johore Province. Another Bren gun barrel lies on the ground next to the weapon. (AWM)

An Australian sentry stands guard at a river in Malaya. The defence of the Muar River was vital to contain the Japanese advance into Johore Province. (AWM)

An Australian 25-pounder field artillery piece with its limber in action under a camouflage net. Allied commanders seldom used this formidable weapon in an anti-tank role and many guns were captured intact by the Japanese in Johore Province. (*NARA*)

An Australian 2-pounder gun crew fires on a Japanese light tank column at a pre-arranged ambush site on the Muar-Bakri Road. Many Japanese light tanks were disabled in this engagement. (*NARA*)

The crew of an Australian 2-pounder gun crew standing at ease after destroying several Japanese light tanks on the Muar-Bakri Road in Johore Province. (NARA)

A column of Australian troops marches past the disabled Japanese tankettes destroyed in action at Milne Bay on New Guinea that were similarly halted by Australian 2-pounder gunfire in Johore Province. (AWM)

A close view of a Japanese Type 95 *Ke-Go* light tank disabled on the Muar-Bakri Road by the concealed Australian 2-pounder anti-tank guns. The tank's main weapon was a 37mm turret gun with two 7.7mm machine-guns, one in the turret and one on the hull. *(NARA)*

The body of a dead Japanese tank crewman lies beside his Type 95 *Ke-Go* light tank after its disabling by Australian anti-tank guns in Johore Province. *(NARA)*

(*Above*) Japanese infantry race across railway tracks at the Gemas station during fighting in Johore Province. (*USAMHI*)

(*Opposite page*) Japanese infantry wait patiently behind a wall of sandbags as one of its accompanying light tanks moves through a street in search of enemy forces in a Johore Province town. (*USAMHI*)

(*Right*) Japanese infantry cautiously advance past a locomotive at the Gemas rail yards during their conquest of Johore Province at the end of the campaign for the Malayan Peninsula. (*USAMHI*)

A Japanese sentry stands on an embankment above a destroyed bridge during the Allied retreat in Johore Province. (*USAMHI*)

An Indian infantry column in Chevrolet 25-cwt light trucks moves to the front during the fighting in Johore Province. Even late reinforcements with the Indian troops could not help General Bennett stem the Japanese advance through this most southern Malayan province. (*NARA*)

General Yamashita and his staff inspect a scene of recent fighting during his victorious sweep through the Malayan Peninsula. His arrival at the Straits of Johore by the end of January had certainly put him ahead of his time table for the conquest of both Malaya and Singapore. (*USAMHI*)

Chapter Five

Defence of Singapore Island

Historically, the civilian population of Singapore had been a polyglot since the late nineteenth century. As mining and rubber estates developed, thousands emigrated from southern China to Singapore Island until they soon outnumbered the Malays. A few Japanese also settled on Singapore Island, making a living as fishermen, small businessmen and shopkeepers. In the mid-1930s, espionage activities among Japanese businessmen and officers (in mufti) were becoming increasingly obvious to the authorities on Singapore Island. In October 1941, there was a mass exodus of Japanese civilians. When hostilities erupted, there was a panic among many of the Europeans on the island that many in the Asian community were fifth columnists or Japanese sympathizers, who believed in the greater East-Asia sphere of prosperity. However, many Malay natives and Chinese residents acted courageously and suffered grievously from the air attacks on the island, which began shortly after war broke out. Notable landmarks on Singapore Island were indiscriminately damaged as well. As news of defeat after defeat on the Malayan Peninsula reached Singapore, evacuation of many European civilians commenced in January 1942.

Percival assumed operational control of all troops on the island and, despite fresh reinforcements, including the Indian 44th Indian Infantry Brigade, the British 18th Division and approximately 2,000 Australians, the situation remained bleak as they were mostly untrained and not acclimatized to the island's weather. Although Percival commanded 85,000 troops to defend a land mass of 220 square miles, 15,000 of them were administrative and non-combatant forces. Also, many units were lacking both adequate weapons and an appropriate *esprit de corps* to combat the Japanese. Percival's intelligence staff officers had clouded their commander's military thinking by estimating that he would be fighting against 65,000 Japanese troops on the other side of the Straits of Johore. The Japanese had to do battle with only 30,000 men. Also, due to less than optimal intelligence gathering, Colonel Tsuji had planned to engage only 30,000 British and Commonwealth troops and not the accurate tally of 85,000 men. Numerically, the defenders had more than enough strength on the island to repel the invasion, particularly as it came where Wavell had expected it to be. In Percival's favour, the island had ample provisions of food and was well-stocked with ammunition for its batteries and troops' personal weapons and machine-guns. Again, there was a complete absence of Allied tanks on the island and an air presence had been destroyed, although as the Japanese had demonstrated on the Malay Peninsula, they were able to land tanks on Singapore Island.

Although Whitehall in London claimed that Singapore was a fortress, its 15-inch naval gun batteries were situated against a possible attack from the sea to the south and east of the island. Also, only a few of the other 6- and 9.2-inch guns that were situated on the south of the island could be swivelled about to fire mostly armour-piercing and not high explosive or anti-personnel shells on the Japanese preparing to cross the Straits of Johore to the north. Once the decision to evacuate to the island fortress was made, Percival failed to take the counsel of both his subordinate commanders and ABDA commander Wavell. In this tactical disagreement between Percival and Wavell, the former opted for an all-round perimeter defence of the island's beaches, whereas the field marshal recommended that he concentrate his forces against the likely Japanese landing sites in most probably the north-west and, perhaps, north-east corners of the island, while also massing some reserves inland for a strong counterattack to throw the invaders back into the Straits of Johore. Percival divided the 27 mile × 13 mile island into three sectors with the Australian 22nd and 27th Brigades in the west; the 28th Indian (Gurkha) Brigade; and the British 18th Division's 53rd, 54th and 55th Brigades in the northern sector and a southern zone to be held by the newly arrived 44th Indian Brigade, along with the Singapore Straits Volunteer Force and the 1st and 2nd Malay Brigades constituting the reserve to the west and east of Singapore City respectively (see map on p. 160–1 for troop dispositions on Singapore Island, February 1942).

Before the war, the Japanese had studied the problem of attacking Singapore Island. The decision was made that the most favourable line of attack, in strength, would be to cross the narrowest portion of the Johore Strait on the north-west coast of the island. The coast of southern Johore province, opposite this area landing area, offered both roads and swampy areas to amass the necessary forces in comparative secrecy. Yamashita's intelligence reports indicated that the British expected the main attack to be hurled against the naval base at Sembawang and that the defences were stronger there than elsewhere. Yamashita, therefore, decided to use his pre-war analysis and make his main thrust with the 18th and 5th Divisions against the north-west coast of the island, away from the main defences of the three brigades of the newly arrived British 18th Division positioned in proximity to the naval base and the north-east section of Singapore Island. Also, Yamashita would make a diversionary attack with the Imperial Guards Division well to the east to deceive the British of the major attack site as well as to offset his numerical inferiority while crossing the Straits. Then, he would deploy the main part of this division to the immediate west of the causeway after the main attack of the Japanese 18th and 5th Divisions had been successfully delivered.

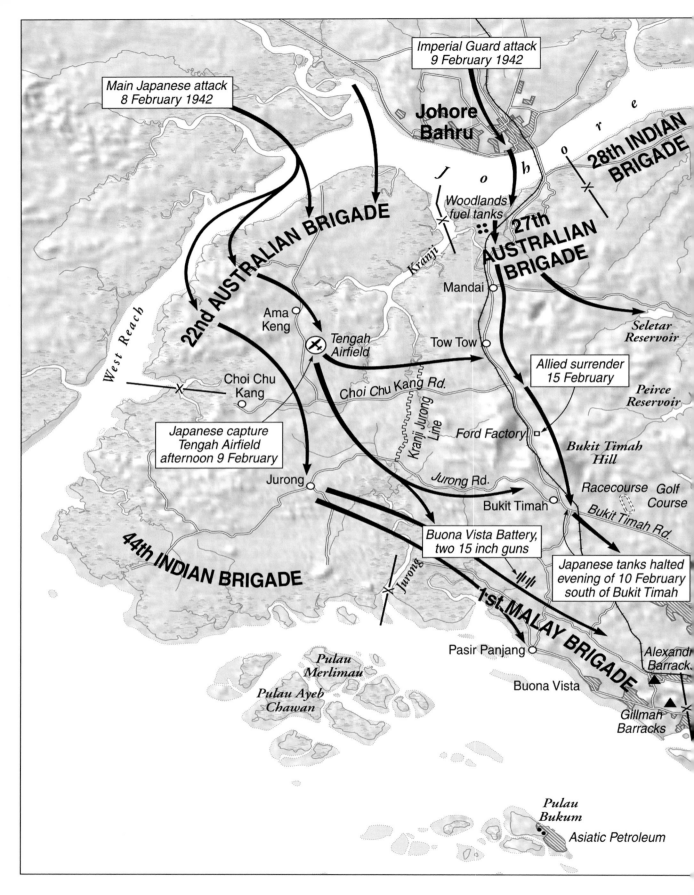

Imperial Guard attack
9 February 1942

Johore Bahru

28th INDIAN BRIGADE

Main Japanese attack
8 February 1942

J   *o*   *h*   *o*   *r*   *e*

Woodlands
fuel tanks

27th AUSTRALIAN BRIGADE

22nd AUSTRALIAN BRIGADE

Kranji

Mandai

West Reach

Ama
Keng

Tengah
Airfield

Tow Tow

Seletar
Reservoir

Allied surrender
15 February

Peirce
Reservoir

Choi Chu
Kang

Choi Chu Kang Rd.

Kranji Jurong Line

Ford Factory

Bukit Timah
Hill

Japanese capture
Tengah Airfield
afternoon 9 February

Jurong

Jurong Rd.

Bukit Timah

Racecourse Golf
Course

Bukit Timah Rd.

44th INDIAN BRIGADE

Jurong

Buona Vista Battery,
two 15 inch guns

Japanese tanks halted
evening of 10 February
south of Bukit Timah

1st MALAY BRIGADE

Pasir Panjang

Buona Vista

Alexandra
Barracks

Pulau
Merlimau

Gillman
Barracks

Pulau Ayeb
Chawan

Pulau
Bukum

Asiatic Petroleum

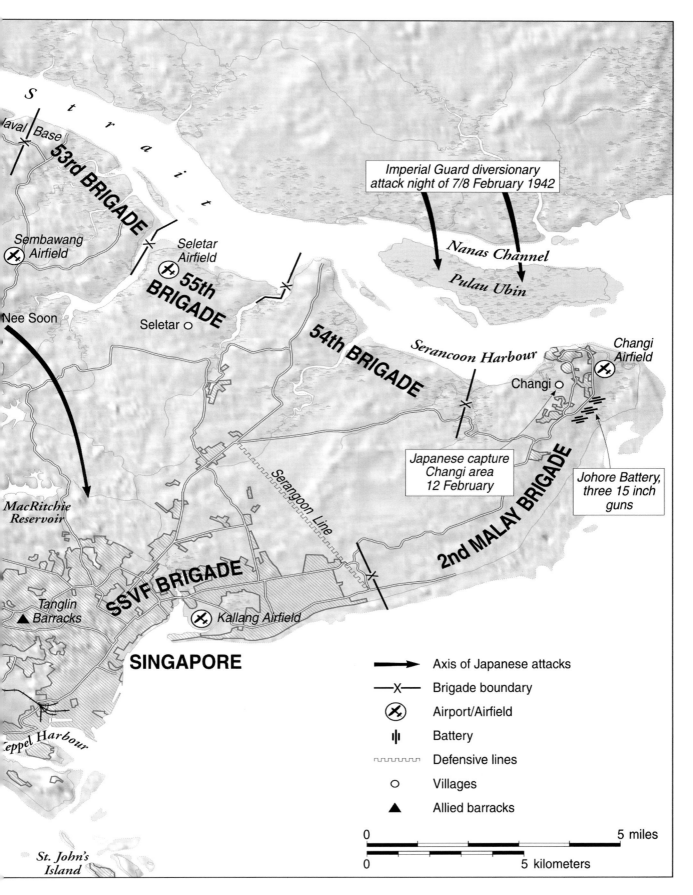

Strait

Naval Base

53rd BRIGADE

Sembawang Airfield

Seletar Airfield

55th BRIGADE

Seletar ○

Nee Soon

MacRitchie Reservoir

Imperial Guard diversionary attack night of 7/8 February 1942

Nanas Channel

Pulau Ubin

54th BRIGADE

Serancoon Harbour

Changi ○

Changi Airfield

Japanese capture Changi area 12 February

Johore Battery, three 15 inch guns

Serangoon Line

2nd MALAY BRIGADE

SSVF BRIGADE

Tanglin Barracks

Kallang Airfield

SINGAPORE

Keppel Harbour

St. John's Island

➡	Axis of Japanese attacks
—X—	Brigade boundary
⊗	Airport/Airfield
�III	Battery
⌐⌐⌐	Defensive lines
○	Villages
▲	Allied barracks

0   5 miles

0   5 kilometers

On 31 January, after the Allies abandoned the Malay Peninsula, Yamashita held a conference with his staff officers and told them that it would take four days to adequately reconnoitre for optimal crossing sites of the Straits of Johore. Concurrent with this were the efforts of the Japanese engineers to repair the destroyed causeway as soon as possible. True to his schedule, on 4 February Yamashita's reconnaissance for the crossing of the Straits was complete. The 25th Army commanding general gathered his divisional commanders at midday on 6 February for their orders. Yamashita had established his headquarters overlooking the now-destroyed causeway in the Sultan of Johore's palace atop a hill. He was certain that the British would never use artillery fire against the Sultan's palace and as an observation post, it offered him a spectacular view of the forthcoming assault beaches on the north-western coast of the island. During the days preceding the Japanese attack across the Straits, Yamashita brought up his artillery, ammunition and supplies using captured railway stock and trucks. He also hid hundreds of folding boats and landing craft for the eventual crossing in the marshy swamp areas about a mile from the Straits.

The Imperial Guards Division began their demonstration attack as planned on the evening and night of 7/8 February. Twenty motor launches containing 400 guardsmen in a very noisy fashion landed on Ubin Island in the Straits overlooking the Changi fortress and airfield, in order to be easily detected by the British troops garrisoning the naval base. On the morning of 8 February, Yamashita's artillery began its bombardment of the Changi fortress as the British, having fallen for the decoy attack, rushed reinforcements to the north-east corner of the island. After the sun had set that day, Yamashita's 5th and 18th Divisions carried their folding boats for over a mile to the Straits' edge. Simultaneous with these troops reaching the water, a massed artillery bombardment commenced on the naval base to destroy its oil tanks, thereby depriving the British the option of setting the Straits ablaze with dumped petrol to combat the amphibious assault, which was a ploy Churchill had planned for the Channel coast if the Nazis had launched Operation *Sealion*. Then, Yamashita's artillerymen turned their guns' attention to Percival's machine-gun nests, infantry trenches and barbed wire below the causeway on the north-west corner of the island. At 2230 hours, 4,000 men in their flotilla of over 300 assorted boats crossed the Straits with artillery, silencing the boats engines to an awaiting 2,500 men of the 22nd Australian Brigade on Singapore's north-west coast. Within minutes of beginning their crossing, elements of the IJA 5th Division were ashore facing heavy Australian machine-gunfire on Singapore Island, while other Japanese troops landed in a mangrove swamp that was less well-defended. In some areas the Japanese had to make three attempts before securing a beachhead on the island. After midnight, the Australians were being attacked from the rear as well as from the water to their front. Therefore, the Australian brigades on the island's north-west coast were unable to hold back the main Japanese invasion, principally due to a lack of ammunition and an adequate counterattacking force formed before the island's invasion. By 0300 hours on 9 February, the entire 22nd Australian Brigade was ordered back to a prepared position. As dawn came, Japanese tanks with fresh 5th and 18th Division infantry arrived in waves totalling roughly 15,000 men and artillery pieces. Once Yamashita had observed that his invading force had reached the Tengah airfield, well inland on the island western side, he crossed the Straits himself. His troops were no further than 10 air miles from Singapore City in the south-eastern corner of the island. Yamashita's assault on Singapore Island possessed surgical precision and efficiency with its feint to the east and the main attack being launched from the west of Johore Bahru town. Also, on 9 February the main elements of the Imperial Guards crossed the Straits immediately to the west of the Causeway, deploying through Johore Bahru town to confront the Australian 27th Brigade. After landing, the Imperial Guards Division was to swing east towards Sungei Seletar and then south to interpose itself between Singapore and Changi, in order to prevent the British withdrawing into the Changi area. This attack was to be carried out by one regiment and a battalion, while the other regiment was kept in reserve. The Japanese 14th Tank Regiment was attached to this division.

On the same day, Wavell, flew from Java to Singapore Island despite the Japanese air supremacy. The ABDA commander railed at both Percival and Bennett for allowing the Japanese to establish a firm beachhead so easily. He issued an order for an immediate counter-attack and reminded the British and Commonwealth officers, 'It is certain that our troops on Singapore Island greatly outnumber any Japanese that have crossed the Straits. We must defeat them. Our whole fighting reputation is at stake and the honour of the British Empire. The Americans have held out on the Bataan Peninsula against far greater odds, the Russians are turning back the picked strength of the Germans, the Chinese with almost complete lack of modern equipment have held the Japanese for 4½ years. It will be disgraceful if we yield our boasted fortress of Singapore to inferior forces [numerically].' Wavell was too intelligent a soldier to ignore the plain reality that the British and Commonwealth forces lacked modern armour and aircraft, and in an antiquated manner allowed the majority of the island's naval guns to be facing in one direction only – the wrong one. Back in Java, the field marshal cabled Churchill, 'Battle for Singapore is not going well […] morale of some troops is not good […] there is to be no thought of surrender and all troops are to continue fighting to the end.' Despite a shred of optimism in Wavell's communiqué, Japanese air attacks continued against a variety of Singapore's assets.

No successful Allied counter-attack was made against the Japanese, as Wavell had insisted upon. Instead Percival made a further tactical error by withdrawing inland toward Singapore City. General Yamashita sensed that the next British defensive site would be located on the hill at Bukit Timah, approximately 2 miles north-west of Singapore City. He attacked on the night of 10 February with his 5th and 18th

Divisions and, although anticipating a desperate struggle for this strategic locale, since it possessed the island's highest elevation just north-west of the racetrack and golf course on the outskirts of Singapore City, confusion among the British and Commonwealth troops led to a rapid loss of the position to the Japanese. In fact, it was elements of the Argyll and Sutherland Highlanders, perhaps Percival's best formation, which found itself caught in the muddle of battle for Bukit Timah Hill and its adjacent supply depots. With the loss of Bukit Timah Hill to the Japanese by dawn of 11 February, space was running out for Percival and his troops. Now the Japanese occupied almost half of the island.

Colonel Tsuji, the offensive's mastermind and chief planner, had made an unsettling observation as to how the British were expending their artillery shells as if they would have no shortage, while Yamashita's artillery ammunition stockpiles were running dangerously low. Perhaps it was Wavell's chiding comments, but to the Japanese commanders the Allied forces having withdrawn inland were putting up a more tenacious fight and Japanese tanks were halted just south of the settlement at Bukit Timah. Some Japanese officers were also concerned that if the British held out for several more days, they would win the battle as Yamashita's ammunition kept dwindling. As an example, Japanese artillery units had to limit their counter-battery fire on British and Commonwealth guns since the former were down to less than 100 rounds per gun. Yamashita's supply system was drained to its utmost limit and he was informed that if fighting continued for another seventy-two hours, he and his forces would be placed in an impossible logistical situation. A few officers had the audacity to even suggest calling off the assault and returning to the mainland for re-supply and re-fitting. However, Yamashita was under intense personal pressure to successfully conclude his offensive as soon as possible to avoid further disfavour from Prime Minister Tojo and other army officers in Tokyo who despised him. Later that day, Yamashita sent a request for surrender to Percival warning him about the potential harm that could come to the civilian population of Singapore City should an all-out assault become necessary.

By 13 February, the retreating British, Australians and Indian troops formed a new 28-mile perimeter around Singapore City. Unfortunately for Percival and his defenders, Japanese artillery destroyed the island's water supply and the attackers had convinced the British that a major epidemic would ensue without fresh water. The capture of the depots at Bukit Timah reduced the island's reserve supplies to just one week. Deserters, refugees and looters were all about the environs of the city. Percival, sensing that there was no panic in Singapore City yet, refused to reply to the surrender request. Like his naval counterpart, Admiral Yamamoto, who was widely known to be excellent at gambling, Yamashita launched into a bluff. He would expend artillery ammunition as if it were unlimited to further convince Percival that he had no alternative but to capitulate. Yamashita instructed his artillery to keep up their fire to suggest to the Allies that the Japanese had an unlimited amount of artillery ammunition. Military deception can sometimes become an added force for a commander willing to employ it at the right time and place.

Forty-eight hours later, Percival had a change of heart. He now sensed a crisis for the civilian and military forces of Singapore City as the Japanese artillery, having put the Seletar, Peirce and MacRitchie Reservoirs out of commission, truly did threaten a drought with its attendant consequences for the city's population. Although trying to exhort his subordinates as conditions looked bleak on this day, Percival conveyed to Wavell that further resistance and loss of life would be futile and that he anticipated not lasting beyond another forty-eight hours. Percival cabled Wavell for permission to surrender. But from ABDA headquarters in Java, the latter refused and urged the island's defenders, 'You must continue to inflict maximum losses on enemy for as long as possible by house-to-house fighting if necessary. Your action in tying down enemy may have vital influence in other theatres. Fully appreciate your situation but continued action essential.'

After meeting with his military commanders on the morning of 15 February, Percival decided to surrender despite a personal message from Churchill to Wavell calling for a last stand by the numerically superior Commonwealth forces. Percival cabled Wavell that he would ask for a cease fire at 1600 hours. Wavell acquiesced and gave permission for the surrender if there was nothing more to be done. Percival had no petrol for vehicles; he had nearly exhausted his field artillery ammunition, since these were essentially the only heavy guns he possessed, and there would be no water in a matter of hours in a city with over 500,000 to 1,000,000 inhabitants living in an equatorial climate. For a personally brave man, such as Percival, capitulation was a bitter step, but he chose to ultimately go himself if called for by the Japanese, in the hope of obtaining better treatment for his troops and the population.

Percival sought terms from General Yamashita on 15 February. Ironically, the capitulation occurred coincident with the evident strain placed on Yamashita's physical and logistical capabilities to continue the offensive causing the 25th Army general to harbour some anxiety. His divisional commanders were now beginning to report severe shortages in ammunition and supplies. Yamashita's chicanery was successful because at 1100 hrs on 15 February, Japanese lookouts saw through the trees along the Bukit Timah road a white flag hoisted atop the broadcasting studios. Lieutenant-Colonel Sugita, one of Yamashita's staff officers at 25th Army headquarters, met a British party seeking to discuss terms of surrender. Sugita told the British officers, 'We will have a truce if the British Army agrees to surrender. Do you wish to surrender?' The British interpreter, Captain Cyril H.D. Wild, agreed with the Japanese officer. Then Yamashita ordered that Percival and his staff come to him in person to the Ford Factory at Bukit Timah.

Six hours after the initial sighting of the white flag, Percival with two staff officers and an interpreter, Captain Wild, met with the 25th Army commander. Negotiations were brief but initially tense. Yamashita wanted an immediate surrender, although Percival was doing his best to stall and keep negotiating the next day. The Japanese 25th Army general knew his actual troop strength and did not want any surrender negotiations delay that might enable the British to discern his true numbers. This fact might embolden Percival to continue the struggle despite his major concerns about water, supplies and the civilian population. After the war Yamashita said, 'I felt if we had to fight in the city we would be beaten.' He went on to discuss that his strategy at Singapore was 'a bluff, a bluff that worked'. At 1950 hours on 15 February, approximately seventy days after invading the Malay Peninsula through Thailand, the surrender document was signed. British and Commonwealth losses in Malaya and on Singapore Island totalled 9,000 killed and wounded with over 120,000 British Empire servicemen taken as prisoners-of-war. The 25th Japanese Army lost approximately 3,000 killed and almost 7,000 wounded. However, one has to remember how the Japanese advanced with almost reckless abandon during the seventy-day campaign that accounted for the greatest military disaster in British history and the greatest land victory in Japanese history.

Japanese male civilians with their families leave Singapore in October 1941. It had been widely known that Japanese spies were acquiring information about Britain's military assets on both the island and the Malayan Peninsula. (*Library of Congress*)

A Singaporean of Chinese ethnicity, serving as an air-raid warden, overlooks Singapore Harbour as fears of an imminent conflict with Japan rise during the late autumn of 1941. (*NARA*)

An air-raid warden on Singapore douses out an incendiary device to demonstrate fire-fighting techniques to an observant crowd one night before the war started. (*Library of Congress*)

During a daytime demonstration, a fire-fighting patrol sprays water on a controlled fire before a crowd in front of a Singaporean department store before the war. (*Library of Congress*)

A Malay rescue crew evacuates the injured from a building in Singapore after an early Japanese air-raid. (*NARA*)

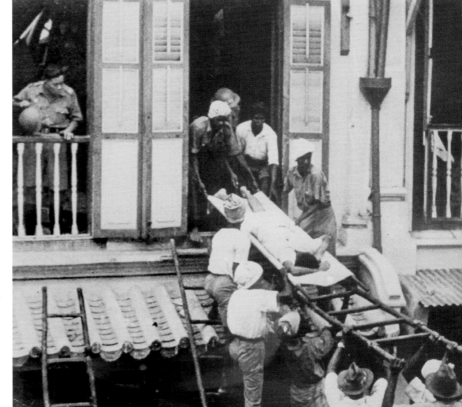

A Malay fire-fighting squad turns its water hose onto flames in a gutted building after a Japanese air-raid in early December 1941. (*NARA*)

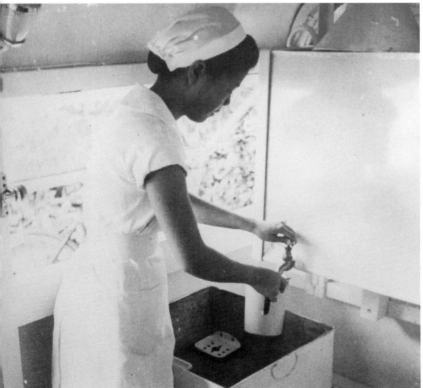

A Malayan girl fills a water pitcher on Singapore Island to comfort those civilians who have lost their homes during a destructive Japanese air-raid. (*Library of Congress*)

Singapore residents, one carrying a newborn in her arms, flee from a burning building on a street that has been devastated by a Japanese aerial bombardment. (NARA)

A glimpse of some of the urban devastation in Singapore after initial Japanese air-raids in early December 1941. (NARA)

Singapore citizens help clear away debris from a destroyed building next to one that remains standing after an enemy air-raid. (NARA)

A Malay civil defence squad carries a wounded citizen on a stretcher. (USAMHI)

Flames burn out of control in a Singapore building while an air-raid warden (*lower left*) watches helplessly. (*NARA*)

Native workers amid smouldering ruins of a Singapore Island district after a Japanese air-raid. (*NARA*)

Malay workers search through Singapore's rubble for survivors after a heavy Japanese attack. (*NARA*)

Ruins of a Chinese store on a Singapore street following a Japanese air-raid. A damaged car is off to the far left. (*NARA*)

173

A crowd of Indians gaze at the debris in front of the Raffles Hotel in Singapore after an early December 1941 air-raid. (NARA)

Throngs of European civilians evacuate Singapore Island in January 1942. Many perished at sea when their ships were attacked and sunk by Japanese aircraft. (*Library of Congress*)

Evacuation of Singapore's European children proceeds from Keppel Harbour in January 1942. Two British soldiers and a seaman stand off to the *left rear* of the trio of children carrying dolls and toys. (*Library of Congress*)

A Gurkha infantryman of the 28th Indian Brigade that was to defend the northern coast of Singapore Island to the west of the naval base carries his Thompson submachine-gun with its drum magazine. (*USAMHI*)

British reinforcements with their kit and rifles on deck about to disembark at Singapore in January 1942 for the defence of the island. (*USAMHI*)

Australian troops disembark from their troopship to reinforce Singapore Island in early 1942. (*AWM*)

Japanese tanks roll down a Singapore street after the surrender in mid-February 1942. The ability of the Japanese to land and transport armour down the Malayan Peninsula and then cross the Straits of Johore was a decisive factor in overwhelming the British and Commonwealth hastily constructed defences. (*USAMHI*)

(*Above*) Members of a Singapore Straits Volunteer Force (SSVF) water-cooled Vickers machine-gun crew defending the southern part of Singapore Island. Percival had many machine-gun emplacements there much to the chagrin of Field Marshal Wavell when he toured the island's defences in January and February 1942. (*Author's collection*)

(*Opposite page*) The first Japanese tanks begin to cross the Straits of Johore to attack Australian positions on the north-western side of Singapore Island after a feint by elements of the Imperial Guards Division to attack the north-eastern portion of the island. (*USAMHI*)

Indian reinforcements stand in formation at Singapore's dockside after disembarking from a troopship. (*Library of Congress*)

A large plume of smoke arises from the naval base at Sembawang far off in the background, as seen from the vicinity of the Municipal Building in the foreground, in February 1942. (*USAMHI*)

Japanese engineers repairing a gap in the Johore Straits causeway to expedite the transport of military vehicles from Johore Bahru, on the southern tip of Johore Province onto the north-western side of Singapore Island in February 1942. (USAMHI)

Japanese troops marching in formation across the Johore Straits causeway. In the background, Japanese engineers are busy repairing the demolished section of the causeway connecting Johore Bahru with Singapore Island. (USAMHI)

Japanese troops coming ashore on the north-western side of Singapore Island from one of their landing barges. The British and Commonwealth troops had strung copious amounts of barbed wire at the water's edge and initially inflicted many casualties on the Japanese amphibious troops. (USAMHI)

(*Opposite page*) Large plumes of black smoke billow upwards from the naval base's fuel tanks. The Japanese wanted to destroy these oil storage tanks to prohibit Percival from setting the Straits of Johore ablaze. (USAMHI)

Japanese 18th Division infantrymen appear silhouetted as they cross the Kranji River in north-western Singapore Island soon after crossing the Straits of Johore on 8 February 1942. (USAMHI)

Japanese infantry with a Rising Sun battle flag crossing Seletar Airfield and stepping over the wrecked wing of a Bristol Bombay, which functioned as a transport aircraft and bomber. (*USAMHI*)

British soldiers and air-raid wardens attempt to put out fires in several trucks at Keppel Harbour after heavy attacl on the southern side of the Singapore Island. (*USAMHI*)

A large cloud of black smoke emanates from a rubber depot at Keppel Harbour several hours after a Japanese air attack. (*USAMHI*)

Civilian workers struggle to douse a fire in a railway yard at Keppel Harbour. (*USAMHI*)

A British merchant ship lists in Keppel Harbour after being struck by bombs. Note the smoke in the background as other parts of the port facility are ablaze. *(NARA)*

Smoke billows from more remote military installations north of the main buildings of Singapore City. *(Library of Congress)*

Japanese infantry lying prone or staying in a crouched posture advance on a burning Singapore Island village. By this time, half the island was under their control. (*USAMHI*)

Japanese troops hurry across a bridge to capture the naval base at Sembawang. Note the civilian car in the foreground. The base was being defended by the 28th Indian Brigade on its western side and the 53rd Brigade (18th British Infantry Division) on its eastern end. (*USAMHI*)

Japanese troops celebrate their capture of the 15-inch British naval guns at the Buono Vista battery on the south side of Singapore Island. (*USAMHI*)

British soldiers and seaman push a civilian car into Keppel Harbour to keep it out of the hands of the Japanese. (*NARA*)

Indian troops with their 3-inch mortar after battle at Bukit Timah, where Japanese tanks were temporarily halted by Singapore Island's defenders in February 1941. (*Author's collection*)

Japanese gunners fire their heavy artillery piece at Singapore installations, even though by the middle of February they were beginning to run low on ammunition. Nonetheless, Yamashita urged them to keep up a steady fire rate. (*USAMHI*)

British Major Harry Flower of the Northumberland Fusiliers negotiates under a flag of truce the return of some of his men who had been captured before the terms of surrender were agreed upon. (*NARA*)

The terms of surrender were negotiated at Yamashita's pace at the Ford Factory at Bukit Timah. Yamashita is facing the camera (*third from left*) while Percival has his back to the camera (*second from left*). Yamashita would not agree to any delay of formal surrender for fear that Percival's staff would find out how few Japanese troops he had and their almost completely expended lot of artillery ammunition. (*USAMHI*)

A Japanese photograph shows Lieutenant-General Yamashita (*third from right*) with Lieutenant-General Percival (*far right*) after the terms of surrender were agreed upon at Bukit Timah on 15 February 1942. (*USAMHI*)

Japanese troops gather to celebrate victory at dockside in Keppel Harbour after Percival's capitulation on 15 February 1942. *(USAMHI)*

Japanese victors make British and Commonwealth troops pose with their hands up for the camera in Singapore on 15 February 1942. (*USAMHI*)

A British cemetery in Singapore with recently interred British troops at the time of the surrender in mid-February 1942. (*Library of Congress*)

Victorious Japanese troops in informal uniform cheerily parade down a Singapore street in front of the General Post Office after the surrender. (*USAMHI*)

Epilogue

Duff Cooper, sent by Churchill to co-ordinate inter-service operations as the resident minister in the Far East, confided to the prime minister that Percival was not a natural leader and could not take a large view. Cooper went on, 'it was all a field day at Aldershot to him [...] he knows the rules as well and follows them so closely and is always waiting for the umpire's whistle to cease-fire and hopes that when the moment comes his military dispositions will be such as to receive approval.' To his many critics, Percival also seemed to lack the requisite ruthlessness to prevail during a military crisis.

So, was it appropriate making Percival responsible for the disaster at Singapore? Many argue that ultimate responsibility for the failure to defend Singapore adequately rests with Churchill, who was often focused on events in the Middle East and diverted important assets to that theatre. General Sir John Dill, as CIGS, wrote to Churchill in May 1941: 'Egypt is not even second in order of priority, for it has been an accepted principle in our strategy that in the last resort the security of Singapore comes before that of Egypt. Yet the defences of Singapore are still considerably below standard.' Even the American military and naval experts endorsed the warning and expressed the view that Singapore should be given priority over Egypt. Factually, the desired air force strength of 300 to 500 modern aircraft was never reached in the Malayan theatre. The Japanese invaded with over 200 tanks, the British Army in Malaya did not have a single one. Indeed, Churchill himself had diverted 350 older model tanks from Malaya to the Soviet Union following the German invasion in June 1941, as a show of good faith between the Allies. As these older infantry and cruiser tanks were more than a match for the light and medium Japanese tanks used in the invasion of Malaya, their presence could well have easily turned the tide of battle on either the Malay Peninsula or Singapore Island.

According to Ronald Lewin, biographer of Archibald Wavell, 'nobody can carp with any justice at an officer who is posted to a position for which he is not suited; the responsibility lies with his superiors or the military secretariat [...] and it was a cruel fate that put him in charge of Singapore's defences.' According to a very harsh critic General Henry Pownall, 'there is no doubt we underestimated the Jap. But suppose we'd made a better show and got the Jap at his true worth, would it have made any real difference? I very much doubt it.'

Atrocities were committed by the Japanese immediately after the surrender and during the lengthy imprisonment and forced labour of the Allied soldiers. When the

Allies liberated Malaya and Singapore after the Japanese surrender, control was taken over swiftly with the enemy usually complacent. Troops of all the Allied forces returned to Singapore Island and the peninsula to re-occupy airfields, military installations and the harbour. Admiral Lord Louis Mountbatten, who eventually succeeded Wavell as the Allied commander in the Far East (also known as Southeast Asia Command or SEAC) conducted the surrender ceremonies of the Japanese at Singapore Town Hall on 12 September 1945, with General Seishiro Itagaki signing the document, as British and Indian troops poured into the island to reclaim it. SEAC had planned to liberate Malaya and Singapore by invading the west coast of central Malaya and advance southwards, Operation *Zipper*, with D-Day being set for 9 September 1945. However, before they could attack, the two atomic blasts at Hiroshima and Nagasaki compelled the Japanese to surrender. After the instrument of surrender was signed, Mountbatten and his entourage left the chamber and took up positions on the terrace before the municipal buildings for the order of the day to be read by the SEAC leader. After that a British flag that had been hidden in Changi jail since February 1942 was run up and Mountbatten gave three cheers for the British monarch. After signing the documents, the Japanese generals were paraded without their swords in front of a jubilant crowd of civilians and military.

While other generals who were held captive by the Japanese, such as the American, General Jonathan Wainwright of Bataan and Corregidor, had become public heroes, Percival found himself disparaged for his leadership in Malaya and Singapore. However, aboard the battleship USS *Missouri*, on 2 September 1945 in Tokyo Bay, Percival and Wainwright stood at MacArthur's side behind the table bearing the Japanese surrender documents. Percival's memoir in 1949, *The War in Malaya*, like its author, was restrained and did not reverse the criticisms of many others. Unusual for a British lieutenant-general, Percival was not knighted for his service to king and country. Percival and Wainwright were also present at another surrender ceremony, in which Yamashita sat opposite them to reverse the humiliation that these two Allied generals had suffered in 1942.

General Percival survived his three-year imprisonment under the Japanese and died in 1966. General Yamashita never suffered at the hands of his political opponent General Tojo and, in fact, commanded the Japanese forces in the Philippines after the fall of Singapore. He surrendered to American forces in the Philippines on 2 September 1945, walking down a mountain path by himself with some of his officers trailing him from his redoubt in northern Luzon. The following day, he and his staff formally surrendered to the Americans in Baguio, Luzon. Yamashita was tried for the atrocities committed in Manila in 1945 and they weighed heavily against him despite the fact that he ordered Japanese troops to leave the city and spare the civilian population from house-to-house fighting. Unfortunately, Rear Admiral Sanji Iwabuchi re-occupied Manila and, with his 16,000 seamen, committed many atrocities against the civilian population along with destruction of all naval facilities and port warehouses. MacArthur made sure that Yamashita's trial was conducted hastily and he was sentenced to death for war crimes. President Truman refused to commute the sentence to life imprisonment. A now gaunt-appearing Yamashita was calm and stoical as he was hanged on 23 February 1946 in Los Banos, a town 35 miles south of Manila.

Within days of Percival's surrender, Wavell returned to India to resume command of that theatre. The Dutch took over the ABDA Command but it too was short-lived with the impending fall of Java to the Japanese, and this onerous command structure was disbanded on 22 February 1942, one week after British and Commonwealth capitulation on Singapore. On 13 June 1943, after helping to successfully create Orde Wingate's Chindits and Operation *Longcloth*, as well as supervising failed invasions of Burma's Arakan region, Wavell was offered the Viceroyalty of India by Prime Minister Churchill, who was searching for a way to graciously remove him as C-in-C India.

Among many other atrocities, a Japanese officer positions his firing squad to execute Sikh prisoners. *(NARA)*

Sikh prisoners sit atop a small knoll blindfolded awaiting execution by a Japanese firing squad. (NARA)

The Japanese firing squad discharges its rifles, each infantryman with a pre-assigned and numbered target. (NARA)

After the firing squad completed it execution duties, a Japanese infantryman with a bayonet attached to his rifle (*left*) and a Japanese officer with a pistol (*right*) kill any survivors of the condemned Sikhs. (*NARA*)

Elements of the RAF Regiment disembark from their troopship at Keppel Harbour to start their march for Kallang Airfield soon after the Japanese surrender in September 1945. (NARA)

Indian troops of the 5th Division cheerily ride through Singapore's streets in open lorries while a local crowd lining the road waves to them. (NARA)

An Indian sentry of the 5th Indian Division stands guards with his Sten machine-gun pointed on Japanese troops standing in front of their former headquarters in Singapore after the surrender in September 1945. (NARA)

A Malay soldier gives directions to 5th Indian Division troops as their officer in charge pores over a map in September 1945. (NARA)

Disarmed Japanese troops walking out of Singapore City while 5th Indian Division soldiers disembark from their lorries in September 1945. (*NARA*)

Japanese officers surrender their swords at a ceremony to both British and Indian officers. (*USAMHI*)

Japanese troops pulling some carts while others walk besides their bicycles loaded with gear on their way out of Singapore City as 5th Indian soldiers look on. (NARA)

A surrendering Japanese officer with his sword still at his side gives directions about Japanese installations to British troops in Singapore in September 1945. (USAMHI)

Admiral Lord Louis Mountbatten, SEAC commander, and Field Marshal Sir Alan Brooke, CIGS, drive to the surrender ceremony at the Municipal Building on 12 September 1945. (*NARA*)

Admiral Lord Louis Mountbatten, SEAC commander, presides over the surrender ceremony as Japanese officers, led by General Seishiro Itagaki, C-in-C of the Japanese 7th Area Army, sitting in the front row sign the documents of surrender. (*NARA*)

Admiral Lord Louis Mountbatten, SEAC commander, reads the order of the day after the surrender documents were signed by the Japanese delegation in the municipal building minutes before this photograph was taken. (*From left-to-right*): Admiral Sir Arthur J. Power, RN; General Sir William Slim 14th Army commander; Mountbatten; General Raymond A. Wheeler, United States Army; Air Chief Marshal Keith Park, RAF and unsung hero of the Battle of Britain. (*NARA*)

General Seishiro Itagaki, C-in-C of the Japanese 7th Area Army, who was subsequently hanged for covering up evidence of Japanese atrocities in Singapore, is flanked by a pair of Royal Navy officers, as the procession exits the Municipal Building, 12 September 1945. (*NARA*)

Admiral Lord Louis Mountbatten, SEAC commander, gives cheers for the king on 12 September 1945 after the signing of the surrender documents and the raising of a British flag that had resided in Changi Prison since 1942. (NARA)

The two adversaries Lieutenant-General Arthur E. Percival and Lieutenant-General Tomoyuki Yamashita sit across from one another at a surrender ceremony in Japan in September 1945. Percival sits to the left of the microphone, while Yamashita is the middle of the three Japanese officers in the foreground. (USAMHI)

General Yamashita, commanding officer of Japanese forces in the Philippines, surrenders on 2 September 1945. He walks by himself in front of his officers from a redoubt in Northern Luzon. (*USAMHI*)

General Yamashita is met by US Army officers as he surrenders his forces in the Philippines on 2 September 1945 in Northern Luzon. (*USAMHI*)

The gaunt, aged Tiger of Malaya, Lieutenant-General Tomoyuki Yamashita, photographed shortly before his execution for war crimes. He was calm and stoical as he was hanged on 23 February 1946 in Los Banos, a town 35 miles south of Manila. (*USAMHI*)